CONVICTIONS

CONVICTIONS

Helping men close the gap between
feeling convicted and living with conviction.

VINCE MILLER

CONVICTIONS
Published by RESOLUTE

Edited by Paul Wonders
Interior Design and Layout by Gretchen Miller
Cover Design by Vince Miller
Cover Layout by Eric Beavers
Printed by Book Villages

ISBN: 978-0-9982133-0-9

Printed in the United States of America

DEDICATED:

To the man who wants to go all-in, but is not sure how

Live with Conviction

TABLE OF CONTENTS

RESOLUTE

CONVICTION

So let me share a single sentence from the Old Testament—words from a different time in our history, but no less striking to our modern ears. Read them slowly and let them wash over you a little bit, and then I want you to consider how they make you feel.

And I sought for a man among them who should build up the wall and stand in the breach before me for the land, that I should not destroy it, but I found none.

Ezekiel 22:30

These words are chilling. If I were to compile a top-ten list of sobering sentences in the Bible, I would put this one close to the top. You might want to read it again:

"And I sought for a man among them who should build up the wall and stand in the breach before me for the land, that I should not destroy it, but I found none."

I have to say, I am so glad that I didn't live in that day and time. Imagine sitting on the bench, out of the game, listening to God's report—but we don't have to imagine. As God speaks this sentence, I can hear the booming echo and feel the resounding vibration of His words across the planet. It is a call for a man. God is looking for a willing man, and He can't seem to find one. Not one. Remarkable, isn't it?

But as I've read these words over the last twenty years in my relationship with Jesus Christ, I've discovered that you can receive these words in one of two different ways. You can either hear God speak them in a tone of disappointing judgment, or you can receive them as a challenge to be accepted. If you choose the latter, then you hear what I hear: God daring me as a man to act boldly as a man.

I believe that God does indeed intend for us to hear this sentence as a challenge, not a rebuke. And within this passage I think God describes the man that He is seeking; in this one sentence, God tells us exactly what He wants from a man. He lays out four distinct qualities:

Quality one – **active**. God's men are men of action. Very simply put, they do something. Instead of worrying about directional perfection, they strive to be directionally correct. God's men are willing to get off the bench, into the game. Such men hate complacency, deplore spiritual idleness, and disapprove of apathy. As God's men we cannot wait for that mysterious day when we'll finally have enough time, schooling, understanding, security, or even enough money. We must act not without thought, but in faith. As Will Rogers understood, "Chaotic action is preferable to orderly inaction."

Quality two – **single-minded**. God's men are entirely focused on God's will, purposes, and desires. This is not a single-mindedness that reflects stubborn self-centeredness, but resolute focus on God, a focus that startles the world. There is something about such men that stimulates our amazement, and demands our admiration. They have devoted themselves to something unequivocally, regardless of the circumstance: If God requires us to stand alone for our faith in front of a jeering and spitting crowd, we must do it. Undeterred by the philosophies of the world and the thoughts, actions, and attitudes of others, as God's men we must stand alone, when God calls, regardless of the consequence.

RESOLUTE

Quality three – **properly aligned**. God's men have their priorities in order, putting God in the highest place. They are consumed by the desire to serve God. And they understand that this often requires putting the needs of others before their own. We must look to God, study His values, and strive to align our values and priorities accordingly. This alignment lets us act boldly, confident in our path, refusing to compromise the mission, goals, or values that God has given us.

Quality four – **all-in**. God is looking for men who are all-in. These men fully understand that God has never been a God of minimums, but maximums. God wants all of us—all our heart, mind, soul, and strength. There is no turning back once a covenant has been made with God, and we are not in an "exclusionary contract" with God. God calls us to give it all we've got, to the very last word, thought, and desire. This is full submission to the Lordship of Jesus Christ, and when we abdicate our self-centered desires, we do so for the benefit of Christ. In submitting your heart to the Triune God, your entire life—including your finances, family, and future—takes a back seat to your renewed mission. This is what it means to become an all-in man.

And herein lies our definition of Godly conviction:

Godly conviction is single-minded and properly alligned belief in God and His truth that produces action and all-in living regardless of circumstances.

Conviction requires the whole being of a man, from his thoughts and attitudes to his actions. And when conviction is undergirded with a God-centered, biblical worldview, it erupts with supernatural force. When the faithful work of an ordinary man is amplified by God Himself, the world will take notice and the powers of darkness had better watch out.

This is the sort of life God wants from us and for us. Maybe it sounds impossibly radical, but God hasn't teased us with an empty challenge. It is an invitation. He is ready to stir conviction within us—a conviction that looks exactly like the one He describes in this passage from Ezekiel. Since I began my relationship with Christ, these words have haunted me, and I hope you, too, can hear the call. God is looking for a man to stand in the breach. The question is, are you that man?

We Must Be Taught Conviction

God has long been looking for men of true conviction. With candidates in such short supply—and all of them flawed—He had to self-provide. In Jesus Christ, we see the magnificent beauty of God's true man. This is what conviction in a follower looks like: a man of action, single-minded, well-ordered, and all-in. But it wasn't enough for Jesus to model the sort of conviction God desires; He went out and taught others how to live as He did.

Somehow, in a little less than two years, Jesus successfully transferred eternal wisdom to a small group of men, helping them to understand the new identity God wanted them—and truly all men—to inhabit. In fact, Jesus Christ was so remarkably good at it, that by the time He ascended, we see that His followers were willing to dedicate every part of themselves for His glory. Acts 4:13 says, "People looked on as Peter and John spoke with such boldness [or conviction]. And people were amazed by it, because they were common, ordinary men." And then the following verse says, "They could tell that they had been with Jesus." Over the course of those two years under Jesus' leadership, they developed a bold conviction unlike anything the world had ever seen. It utterly transformed their thoughts, attitudes, and actions to the point that they radiated Christ Himself. And I have got to tell you, that's exactly what I want my life to look like. I want people to see not me, but Christ in me. This is what I desire, what I pray you also desire: to live a life of real conviction.

But Do We Live With Conviction?

If you are holding this book and have read this far, I assume you share the desire to live with conviction, but don't know how to actually do it. I meet men every day who are stuck in this very struggle. There are a host of reasons for this gap between desire and outcome, but here are four of the most common factors:

First, a great majority of men feel that they lack a leader, and the subsequent accountability, to guide them on this journey toward conviction. This was definitely true for me. I can confidently say, having served as a pastor for the last two decades, that this is a major issue in our church; men want to engage in discipleship, but fail to find a leader to guide them. This is not a new problem. In the first pages of the New Testament Gospels, we see how the twelve disciples lacked a "Rabbi" in their lives until Jesus came along. On my own journey with Christ, I have often sought other men who might lead me in discipleship, but they often protested that either they didn't have the time, or they didn't know how to lead me. This leadership void is a critical problem that breaks down the whole discipleship process. Jesus was crystal clear in his final call to His disciples in Matthew 28. The call to "make disciples" was not a suggestion, recommendation, or nice idea—it was a mandate of utter importance to the survival of the message and Christianity itself. Failure to follow through is catastrophic for future generations.

Second, some men are so ashamed of their own sin, and patterns of repetitive sin, that they can barely imagine living with conviction. I witness this frequently. When conviction seems like an impossibility, willpower dissolves into despair. The continued lack of spiritual stamina and isolation from resources only reinforces slavery to sin. Emotionally this results in a cycle of shame and regret that will only detach them further from healthy Christian community. And even though I plead with these men to engage with God, every move towards them leads to a countermove of renewed resistance. And here we learn the reality of these words from John Owen: "Be killing sin, or it will be killing you."

Third, some men don't live with conviction because they simply don't know the path of repentance. They struggle to reconcile with God when they feel so far from God. A healthy understanding of repentance pushes men toward a life of conviction, just as a lack of understanding keeps them away. Because only through repentance can men find reconciliation and restoration in their relationship with God and others.

Fourth and finally, many men don't live with conviction because they sense that their purpose, mission, and very identity are out of alignment. Perhaps they feel otherwise healthy, but cannot find real purpose. The pursuit of a successful career feels meaningless, and now they're asking the bigger questions. How can their identity connect with God's purpose?

What all these men have in common is that they have become convicted—and are stuck in that miserable state. How can they take the next step forward, towards the exhilarating life of conviction?

We spend our lives feeling and being convicted yet living without conviction.

But this is not a new topic; again we can turn to the Gospels, where in Matthew 7:24–27 Jesus says this:

"Everyone then who hears these words of mine and does them will be like a wise man who built his house on the rock. And the rain fell, and the floods came, and the winds blew and beat on that house, but it did not fall, because it had been founded on the rock. And everyone who hears these words of mine and does not do them will be like a foolish man who built his house on the sand. And the rain fell, and the floods came, and the winds blew and beat against that house, and it fell, and great was the fall of it."

Jesus here is explicit about conviction. What you have are two types of men. You have men who hear and don't do, who are characterized as foolish; these are those who are being convicted but do nothing. On the other hand, you have men who both hear and do, who are characterized as wise, and who live in conviction. Both are building a life, apparently using similar techniques, but on two different foundations. What exposes both men is the trial—in this case the storm—that reveals how well they have integrated what they have heard with what they do. The trials reveal their conviction. And we all know this is always true.

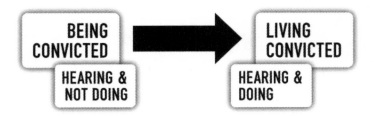

God is looking for men of conviction. Not just one or two spiritual outliers, but a multitude that will bless churches, homes, and workplaces across the world. You know you can stand to live with more conviction in some area of your life. You also know that you cannot afford to not make changes that deepen your knowledge and action on those convictions. As men, when we grow in this way, everyone wins. This book will help you prepare for the adventure that follows. We will study and learn to follow the pattern of Jesus Christ, The Resolute Man. May you discover the conviction you seek in your relationship with Him.

The Content

Here at Resolute, we know that men are always looking for tools to grow in their faith. One of our big goals is to equip you. We long to put tools and resources into your hands that aid you in becoming the man you want to be: a man that influences his home, family, workplace, and church. These resources have been designed for your use both individually and in a group. We believe it is men like you who will influence the kingdom, and we want to be part of your path to influence.

This book is separated into four sections, each covering a primary factor that can provoke within you a deeper conviction than you've ever experienced before. At the conclusion of each chapter, you will find links to resources that will help you and your men's small group dig further into these ideas and principles. These include the following:

- A printable Resolute Study Guide that supports the chapter. It contains group questions, biblical text for study, and various thoughts for private study or discussion in your men's group.
- A weekly Accountability Report guide. This tool is designed for weeks of ongoing discussion that will aid you in building accountability into your life with another man. Several weeks' worth of discussion topics are included on a single printable guide.
- Access to a Podcast and Video Curriculum. There are four podcasts and videos, one for each chapter of this book. You can choose to listen or watch this chapter on your own or as a group, and I will be your small group leader for a 60-to-90-minute session. This gives you a sample of our premium year-long program called the Resolute Cohort, which contains 48 weekly sessions and guides men through a very robust discipleship and leadership experience.

Whether you're part of a Resolute Cohort or a traditional men's small group, these additional study resources will help you help each other along the road to true conviction. And if you currently are not part of such a group, I would highly encourage you to find a couple of other men to do this study with; reading solo is fine, but you will get the most out of these materials in a group setting.

Be resolute,

Vince Miller
Founder
RESOLUTE
WWW.BERESOLUTE.ORG

ACCOUNTABILITY

It was accountability that Nixon feared.

Bob Woodward, Journalist

You're feeling convicted. It's a miserable state, and you want out. Just out of reach, you see a different life waiting for you. One of significance and purpose. The problem is, you can't get there on your own strength. If you want to live your live with conviction, you're going to need to get some accountability.

The Story of Accountability

I grew up in the San Francisco Bay Area and I lived there until I was in my young 20s. During this time, I was exposed to a number of great sporting venues. Very close to my home, I had access to both the Oakland Coliseum and Candlestick Park. I loved going to games in Oakland as a kid, watching the Athletics and the Raiders—even if the Raiders games could get a little rowdy. And just across the bay, games featuring the 49ers and the Giants were also a blast. I grew up with these sporting heroes that were bigger than life to a young teen. Rickey Henderson, who could steal bases with unbelievable speed; Joe Montana, who could evade every defender and complete any pass; and of course Jerry Rice, who with his web-like hands and leaping power could make the impossible catch. But as you get older, your perspective on your childhood heroes will likely change. Sometimes they disappoint you with poor behavior or the revelation of a scandal; such was the case with many of these "heroes."

But sometimes as you learn more about the person off the field or out of the spotlight, your opinion of the person can actually improve.

A few years ago, I was watching an interview with one of my childhood heroes, quarterback Steve Young. Steve had just been inducted into the NFL Hall of Fame, and he was being interviewed at a formal gathering. They asked him the reason for the success he had enjoyed throughout his football career. And he said this one word: accountability.

I perked up immediately as Young clarified, "It's not about accountability itself. It was about my willingness to accept accountability." (Did you catch that phrase? Again: Willingness to accept accountability.) Young talked about his move into the NFL, those first experiences on a professional stage, and how he came to understand that some things had to change in his life. And his decision to embrace accountability was perhaps the greatest contributing factor to his success. This single principle significantly improved his career in three areas: his performance on the field, chemistry with the team, and his leadership of the team.

At this point in the interview, I said aloud to myself, "I want all those things." I want to perform better on the field of life. I want to have better chemistry with my team and family. I want to be more respected by the people I lead. So Young had my full attention as he shared openly about his initial lack of willingness to be held accountable. He admitted that early in his career, upon throwing an interception—the worst mistake a quarterback can make on the field—he responded adversely to others, rather than taking responsibility for his own miscues. Let me assure you, this type of personal admission of fault is something you rarely hear from men in his position.

Young had to learn to be willingly accountable for the interceptions that he threw in life. He was in a bad pattern of blaming what he called all the "mitigating circumstances" that led to an interception, rather than owning the mistake himself. Bad pass protection from his offensive linemen led to a tipped ball, or maybe a wide receiver ran to the wrong spot on the field; had everyone else been doing their jobs, Young felt, his interceptions never would have happened.

You can laugh, but we've all been there, right? "I had to learn to willingly accept accountability," said Young, "and stop blaming the mitigating circumstances. And when I did, everything changed. My performance went up, because I owned it. The team liked me more because I was owning it." And he attributed this new attitude as the greatest contributing factor to his success in comeback victories. By refusing to blame his teammates in the most dire game situation, and in fact claiming personal responsibility, he inspired him teammates to play harder, with greater focus. And so Young was able to lead his team to new heights.

Listening to that interview, I was so drawn in by Young's case for willing accountability. But here's the thing: I've stepped out onto the field of the old Candlestick Park, and from that perspective you'll immediately understand that Young could not have escaped accountability even if he wanted to. Because it was all around him every game day and every day between. There were 60-80,000 fans watching him from every single angle. Twenty to thirty coaches carefully studied every second of every play, listening to every call and every decision that he made. And all the while, video cameras documented everything, able to play back every moment in slow motion, second by second. They exposed all his weaknesses for what they truly were. By initially denying his plainly visible mistakes, Young lost credibility and respect among the men he was supposed to lead.

Of course, very few of us live our lives in front of a crowd of thousands scrutinizing our every move. Perhaps an NFL quarterback has no choice but to embrace accountability if he wishes to have success, but what about the rest of us? What is at stake for us?

Even though we may not play in a stadium before spectators, we do have an audience. Our family, friends, neighbors, co-workers, and members of our church are spectators to the game of our life, watching our every move. They see who we are through our conversations and interactions, and while we may not realize it, they understand who we are, often better than we understand ourselves. And through their perspective we can find the truth and accountability we need to live with conviction. Our credibility and respect, the very tools you have for effective leadership, are at stake. All men are leaders in some area of life. Let the reality of your leadership responsibilities sink in as you ponder accountability.

Non-Negotiables of Accountability

Men, if you want to live your life with more conviction, then you have to embrace accountability. I have seen this transformation happen in my life and in the lives of others, and I can tell you that even the first small steps towards accountability can produce huge results in a man's life. Those first two steps you will take are difficult, but completely non-negotiable:

- Accept the truth, and stop mitigating.
- Establish an environment of accountability.

To illustrate the importance of this first step, let's look at a story in 2 Samuel 11–12, which centers on King David. After twenty years of righteous ruling, David has sinned. Badly. Perhaps you know the details: A palatial rooftop stroll. An accidental glimpse of a bathing woman in the town below.

An illicit summons to the king's chambers. Pregnancy. Panic. Betrayal. Murder. As the dust settles, a man is dead and his widow—pregnant with the king's son—enters David's harem. In this moment of sin, God is not going to let David off without consequence. So He calls to Nathan the prophet, commanding Nathan to go to David and rebuke his sin.

Nathan could have simply confronted David with a blunt appraisal of his actions, but instead he tells David a story that plays to the king's heart and sense of justice. In the midst of this encounter, we see the most beautiful picture of accountability in the entire Bible. This is it. One man looking at another man and telling the truth. So here's the story Nathan told:

"There were two men in a certain city, the one rich and the other poor. The rich man had very many flocks and herds, but the poor man had nothing but one little ewe lamb, which he had bought. And he brought it up, and it grew up with him and with his children. It used to eat of his morsel and drink from his cup and lie in his arms, and it was like a daughter to him."
(2 Samuel 12:1–3)

Okay. Let's pause and address the obvious weirdness of this furry little story here. Nathan could be describing a cat. At least that's what it sounds like. Or if you don't like cats, which I don't, he could be talking about any other household pet. But the point is, this man has had a very intimate relationship with his pet for a really long time.

"Now there came a traveler to the rich man, and he was unwilling to take one of his own flock or herd to prepare for the guest who had come to him, but he took the poor man's lamb and prepared it for the man who had come to him."
(2 Samuel 12:4)

Yes, this twisted neighbor stole, cooked, and ate another man's pet.

"Then David's anger was greatly kindled against the man."
(2 Samuel 12:5)

Now we need to pause here and notice that David has grown embittered and angry. And he's so angry he interjects into the story. There are two things that are interesting here. First, that he pronounces a judgment as if the story is real! Second, that he couldn't tolerate the same sort of injustice that he himself had perpetrated. Often we feel a deep sense of injustice when we see other people committing the very sins that entrap us. Fascinating, right?

So David interrupts and pronounces judgment:

"As the Lord lives, the man who has done this deserves to die, and he shall restore the lamb fourfold, because he did this thing, and because he had no pity."
(2 Samuel 12:5-6)

And then Nathan completes his entrapment of the king with one of the most chilling lines in the Bible:

"You are the man."
(2 Samuel 12:7)

Ouch.

I bet you know what that feels like. Not a fun moment. See how Nathan finds a way to use the narrative against David, baiting the king into being angry with himself. Nathan continues, explicitly declaring God's judgment—and David gives a remarkable response.

David said to Nathan, "I have sinned against the Lord."
(2 Samuel 12:13)

This is a beautiful story of accountability. Nathan illustrates the thoughtful Spirit-inspired calling to hold someone accountable, and David demonstrates what willing accountability looks like. I believe that David's response in the middle of this "care-frontation" is an example of a heart that's willing to accept the truth about himself. Having talked to many men in the aftermath of being caught in sin, I suspect there was probably some sort of relief in David's soul. When you are stuck in sin, there is relief in being busted, because that means you don't have to keep living in an unhealthy psychological state of denial and dishonesty. David understood that he could not escape God, couldn't escape the truth—and neither can we.

David was a great warrior, and the Bible is full of stories about his military exploits, but I believe that this is the greatest battle that David ever fought—the battle with himself. Not the childhood battle with a lion and a bear. Not the victory over Goliath. Not the numerous wars that he fought as Israel's king. No, David's greatest battle was to set aside his pride, confront his own sin, and face the truth of God.

Men, hear me in this: our hearts do not want to accept the truth about our own sinfulness. And it takes an epic battle to turn your heart and say, "Regardless of who I am, the mistakes I've made, I'm now going to rotate my heart and I'm going to turn it toward Christ. Not just toward accountability, but toward the willingness to accept the truth. The Truth. Because I can no longer hide from myself." I think this is an amazing feat, more impressive than slaying giants.

But for most of us, what we end up doing is exactly what Steve Young did for years: We mitigate our circumstances.

That is our impulse, to mitigate. To give excuses, to blame, deflect —whatever it takes. And I know it to be true, because I've seen it even in my own life.

A few years back on July 4th, our neighbor Joe invited us over to his home for the usual weekend get-together. Everybody in our neighborhood was heading over to Joe's house. Every year he hosts a big celebration in his backyard, cooking burgers, brats, and chicken. And every year he buys fireworks—and in bigger quantities every successive year. Ready for a fireworks safety story?

Now, usually Joe and one of his brothers would light off the fireworks, but somehow he had coerced me into doing it that year because none of his brothers could come. I had no interest in touching the fireworks, but Joe was insistent, so there I was, setting them on a pedestal in the yard and lighting them off. And with every box Joe handed me, he kept saying, "It's going to get bigger, Vince. Just watch, it's going to get bigger." And he just kept handing me box after box. I didn't even know what most of it was.

We were approaching the grand finale, and I began to feel a little dread because the boxes kept getting bigger, impossibly bigger. Then Joe handed me a square box, all black; there were no labels in sight. Not one. I said to him, "What is this?" He said, "I don't know. Light it."

I set the box on the stand, and I lit the fuse. Just as the fuse was starting to sink into the box, Joe came over and stood next to me, leaning his shoulder against mine. "Vince, did you set that on there right?" And I said, "What do you mean, 'did I set that on there right'?" And then we both looked at each other with great shock and horror.

We turned to the box just as the fuse went in. And the seconds ticked by slowly until we found out whether it

///RESOLUTE

was in the proper position. One-one-thousand, two-one-thousand...

Phoof, phoof—out came these two giant cannons. And instead of bursting up into the sky, they flew straight away from us, horizontal to the ground. The projectiles blasted through a neighbor's wire fence, through another wire fence, and through another, finally exploding in the backyard of one of the few neighbors not at the party. Needless to say, these were not small fireworks; they were designed to shoot about 1,000 feet in the air, making those spectacular displays that we all enjoy. Everybody in attendance was laughing at me—from the kids to the local sheriff!

But what they didn't understand was that this mystery box had recoiled, tumbling off the stand and onto the ground. The sky and yard were dark, making it impossible get a good look at the solid black box that was about to fire a second time. I looked up for Joe and Joe was gone. Like a game of Russian fireworks roulette, I tried to make a quick determination of the direction the box was facing. Too late. Phoof, phoof, phoof— three more large cannons fired out of the mystery box, now aimed into the park preserve along the back of Joe's property. A 90-degree turn.

That blast had come much closer to the guests. All laughter instantly turned into screaming. Kids were running, the sheriff was lying down behind his canvas folding chair, and a couple of elderly neighbors were trying to get into the house.

And still Joe was nowhere to be found. I was standing by myself, looking at the vague black box on the ground, clueless as to which way was up. Another one went off—Phoooof—a big one. This time directly at the crowd. It went right through the back of the sherrif's canvas chair, right over his head, hitting a retaining wall on the other side of Joe's yard and exploding the wall into three large pieces. (Yes, I almost shot the sheriff!) And then I just kicked the box. Out of a desperate impulse to do something, I kicked the box, hoping it might land in a better position. An instant later, the box fired again—and the remaining twenty cannons zoomed safely skyward.

I sat down in my chair, shaking, literally about to throw up. My mistake could have seriously hurt somebody.

Joe walked over, asking, "What happened?"

Instinctively I blurted out, 'You must have handed me the box wrong."

He said, "What? You're going to blame this on me?"

And it took me a second to catch myself mentally. "No, no, it's my fault. I made the mistake."

For the few years since, the walk to Joe's house for the 4th of July celebration has been a walk of shame. And you'd better believe I haven't lit a firework since.

This may be a funny story (yes, I can laugh at it now), but it illustrates how we all mitigate circumstances in our life. We do this mostly because we don't like the truth about us. We don't like to say, "I did that," or "I made a mistake." We have trouble owning our issues and sins.

But God wants a willing heart. He wants someone who will say, "I willingly accept the truth about me." You see, God is all about truth. Truth and accountability go hand in hand. Men, we have to stop making excuses for our failings, and we've got to start accepting the truth, even when we don't like it.

RESOLUTE

If you stopped mitigating and started accepting the truth, imagine the change that would happen in your life. When Steve Young got a taste of that transformation, he learned that if he could just be willing to accept accountability, he could acheive incredible outcomes in his career. For us, of course, as disciples of Christ, the stakes are much higher.

If you became more willing to accept the truth, think about how the people in your life would view you differently. How would your wife view you differently? How would your kids connect with you? How would your employer appreciate you? How might your employees respond to your transparency and honesty? I mean, forget that it's a biblical principle for just a moment. Just consider the relational dividends and the payoff. The potential is beautiful. So why not give it a spin?

Men that live their life with conviction believe that there is an absolute truth, and they're willing to go all-in with that truth. Because God is all about truth.

So in the move toward accountability, we must accept the truth and refuse to mitigate our circumstance. But there's another non-negotiable requirement of accountability: We must establish an environment of accountability.

When Steve Young shares his story, you can almost hear the small voice in his head saying, Steve, you can't escape accountability. You can't. It's so engrained in your life that you can't run away from it. Early in his career, he resisted, and saw the damage he was doing to his team and his career. The Tampa Bay Buccaneers—one of the worst teams in the league at the time—gave up on him, trading him to the San Francisco 49ers in 1987. His attitude could have led him further down the same path until he got dumped again, which is typically what happens to such people in the professional sporting arena. If it's a repeating pattern, then they become unhirable. Their agent might push for another trade or a "change of scenery," but they cannot escape themselves, and cannot break through until they become willing to confront the truth about themselves. Surely you can think of examples of sports figures who never figured it out. They stubbornly refused accountability until one day they found themselves without a career.

A willing heart is necessary to achieve real breakthrough, but willingness is only part of the process. Accountability demands an environment where we have someone to be accountable to.

Do you suppose that Steve Young would have been able to perform at a Hall-of-Fame level without 80,000 fans, thirty coaches, and thirty cameras around to keep him on track? His pressurized environment pushed him to greater excellence. He saw that he had access to consistent, persistent voices offering instruction and exhortation—and he took full advantage. He didn't see accountaiblity as a threat, rather an opportunity to further develop his craft to a Hall-of-Fame level. Had Young's coaches and teammates been subpar across the board—foolish, unknowledgable, unskilled—less would have been required of him. Their low standards and low expectations could have sabotaged Young's career just as much as his initial pride and arrogance. So we see that accountability draws equally from a willing heart on one side and intentionally structured environments on the other.

Everyone knows that accountability drives results. Hear me carefully: as we get better at living in accountability, we begin to accomplish bigger and better things. Every boss knows this, every coach knows this, but somehow the church doesn't. Perhaps you've observed the same disconnect. For some reason, in the spiritual "game of life"—which is the most important "game" we will ever play—we completely lack accountability. And we wonder why we don't live life with

RESOLUTE

conviction. You know what we prefer over accountability? We prefer anonymity, ambiguity—but not accountability. And you know in your heart that it's true.

Anonymity lets us walk in and out of the church without anybody ever knowing who we are, never having to develop a single meaningful relationship. Ambiguity lets us say, "I don't know if such-and-such is wrong, so I can't be guilty." This is indeed a comfortable way to live. Comfortable, and impotent. But accountability, even small amounts of it, will drive us to new levels of spiritual conviction in our relationship with Christ. I have seen it happen. Acceptance of the truth, rejection of your excuses, combined with a community that sees you and will faithfully hold you to God's highest standards—put it all together and you have a discipline that your comfortable self will hate. But it's exactly what your heart needs. This accountability will change the most important areas of your life.

An environment of accountability is the one thing we don't want or have time for that we need the most.

Gentlemen, we have to address our field game. We have to. If you want to live life with conviction, you're going to have to change your game. You're going to have to get some built-in environments of accountability, because God created within us the need for these types of relationships. From the beginning of the Bible to the end, accountability saturates the text as the biblical principle that has perhaps the most potential to bring about change. Seriously. We may have missed it, but the Bible is saturated with illustrations of the power of accountability.

Just turn to the first chapters of the Bible. God gives Adam and Eve one rule, they break it, and He holds three people accountable. Adam, Eve, and Satan. You know why? Because accountability and truth go hand in hand. For God to be truthful, He has to hold us accountable without respect of the person or being. And we can follow this same topic all the way to the end of the Bible. In Revelation 22:12–13, God says, "Behold, I am coming soon, bringing my recompense with me, to repay each one for what he has done. I am the Alpha and the Omega, the first and the last, the beginning and the end."

So you'd better believe that God is all about accountability. Yet for some reason we fail to structure it into our lives. If that's the case in your life, you need to do something about this immediately. Find spiritual accountability. Don't make excuses. Don't hesitate.

We challenge every man that sits in on one of our weekly Resolute Cohorts sessions to pursue accountability, to implement it even in small ways in his life. We want men to walk out of the room saying, "I need to do something about _____ in my life."

This strategy can be deployed anywhere. It can be fostered in a small-group experience or between just two men as they sit across from each other and ask each other the simple but hard questions—it honestly doesn't need to be more complicated than that. The Resolute Accountability Guide provides a list of helpful questions, and I would recommend checking out the web address at the end of the chapter. But if you don't have a person in your life that you can talk to honestly—if you're sitting in your chair right now and you just can't think of a name—you have to change that. It is for this reason that God sent Nathan to David. David couldn't hide in the silence of his solitude any longer once another godly man entered the room.

Find someone to be accountable to, and all of a sudden the field dynamics change, and the likelihood of success goes up by huge percentages. This is not a rhetorical challenge; this is a biblical mandate: if you do not have someone in your life right now who will sit down with you and listen to you and challenge you, you need to address this problem immediately.

So here are the big questions that we need to address to put us on the path to true accountability:

- Who is someone that holds you accountable?
- What do they do to hold you accountable?

Based on my work with Christian men, I have found that most cannot answer the first question, and this is devastating to their pursuit of a life of conviction. If we don't get serious about creating an opportunity for accountability, then we are going to have serious problems now and in the future. The lack of accountability is the foremost contributing factor to hindered spiritual growth. It is stopping many men in their tracks in their quest to become God's man. Is it stopping you?

Finding an Accountability Partner

So we have discovered that accountability will pay huge dividends in living a life of conviction. Like Steve Young, we need eyes on our game, and this is provided by finding the right man who is willing to keep his eyes on us. Again: not just any man, but the right man. While this sounds simple, it can sometimes be hard to find a willing candidate; and once we find him, he will need to understand the ground rules.

So let's begin by identifying the person. Below is a short list of baseline attributes I would look for in a man who could potentially be an accountability partner:

- He has godly character.
- He reads God's Word.
- He can be confidential.
- He cares about God's best interest for your life.
- He feels freedom to challenge you.
- He has relationship chemistry with you.
- He is more mature than you in areas you want to develop.

As you think of someone or consider asking someone to step into this role for you, remember that he will not have all the qualities listed above. This is acceptable because we are all imperfect (but having none or only one of the above qualities would be a deal breaker for me). Remember, the worst decision we can make is to do nothing, so even that inital step of agreeing to a relationship of this type will be a game changer for both of you. I have seen situations where men discuss the list above and then this list becomes the basis of their accountability conversation for the first few weeks. For example, Dave was a friend of mine who was interested in becoming accountability partners with me, but felt that he was not in God's Word enough to validate a partnership of this kind. However, he did have a strong desire to grow spiritually, so my first challenge for him was to regularly read the Word.

So feel free to begin by discussing these seven attributes, and as you move forward, the dynamics will become more advanced.

RESOLUTE

Take a moment to write down the name of a man who exhibits the qualities listed:

The Two Roles of Accountability

Now that you have identified a potential person of the right quality, both you and your partner need to understand the two roles of an accountability relationship, since each man will perform both roles. At any given time, one of you must be the leader, and the other a participant.

Let's begin with the role of the leader. This person focuses on the goal of bringing about successful change in the other man's life. This entails four critical responsibilities. The leader has to be:

- **One** | Motivated by love.
- **Two** | Courageous enough to challenge.
- **Three** | Able to identify key behaviors to change.
- **Four** | Able to check in with good questions.

These four critical responsibilities will make accountability effective. Let dive a little deeper.

First, you have to genuinely love the person you are holding accountable. Love as a motive is perhaps the most powerful tool for personal change. It takes time to build a mutual understanding of how each person uniquely communicates this love, but as you get to know each other over weeks and months, your motives will become more obvious to the other person and will be critical in inciting change in the man you are meeting with. You will care enough about each other to look to one another's best spiritual interests.

This principle is powerfully illustrated through the story of Jesus' interaction with a rich young ruler. Jesus had set out on a journey, and as He was making His way, a man ran up to Him. Falling down before Jesus, the young man asked Jesus a question: "What must I do to inherit eternal life?" Jesus very politely interacted with him, correcting him a little, and then the young ruler responded with a rote answer that all devout followers knew: "Do not murder, Do not commit adultery, Do not steal, Do not bear false witness, Do not defraud, Honor your father and mother." All of these were simple commands very familiar to Jewish boys; I can just see the young man gleaming. But the young man was simply not ready for what Jesus was about to hit him with next—a call for one more level of obedience: "Sell all and give it to the poor." Of course the young man met this request with disappointment, and walked away disheartened and sad because he had great wealth. But there is one very beautiful detail in this story. These words are often missed, yet very relevant from Jesus' point of view: "And Jesus, looking at him, loved him, and said to him..." (Mark 10:17–22).

This is what a great leader does. He loves, in the best way possible. He loves by gently calling out the right words, in the right time, and with the right tone.

Brotherly love in the Greek language is the word philadelphia. Paul in the New Testament used this word a number of times to reference what love looked like between brothers in Christ. Here is one reference from his book to the Hebrew people that explains the forward momentum of love in a relationship between brothers: "Let brotherly love continue" (Hebrews 13:1). Love is the ultimate motivation behind the accountability relationship, which will grow in intensity over time as trust is built.

MOTIVES	**CHALLENGE**	BEHAVIOR	CHECK–IN

Your second responsibility as a leader is to courageously challenge. Like a coach on the sideline, sometimes you will supportively encourage, and sometimes you will courageously challenge.

> *Like a coach on the sideline, sometimes you will supportively encourage, and sometimes you will courageously challenge.*

A leader cannot simply sit back and accept everything his accountability partner will think, say, and do. After you establish your relationship, you have to challenge. If you don't do this early in the relationship, it will become harder to muster the strength to do it as time moves on. So engage in challenge early and often. It is important that you use respectful phrases that can become mutual accountability language. Key phrases include statements like, "I am not sure I agree with you," or "I understand what you are saying, but I respectfully disagree," or "I don't think that is a good idea for you based on what I know about you and this situation."

Remember, you want to be respectful, but not passive; direct, but not cruel. And the more you understand each other, the more effective your challenges will become.

You have to agree early on that there will be times you are going to disagree with an approach or choice, and find a direct yet inoffensive way to signify this challenging moment. Without this agreement to challenge each other, accountability will not have its full punch. You will simply be two guys meeting together, which is a nice gesture, but not an effective use of accountability time.

Your third responsibility as a leader is to remember that while accountability is about behavior change, it is not about all behaviors. When we engage in real accountability, real change will be fostered—but often accountability relationships struggle to focus on the right behaviors.

Accountability is about behavior change but it is not about all behaviors.

We can debate whether or not behaviors are a leading or lagging indicator of a deeper change happening within a person's heart, but the key is that both transformations happen together. As an accountability leader, when you focus on the right behaviors that need to change, you will get to the heart of the motivational issue at hand. And so you will help your friend change his behavior for the right reasons.

RESOLUTE

Accountability is a tool that brings about change in behavior. Focusing on the right behaviors that need to change will lead to the behaviors changing for the right reasons.

Once a leader proves that he is motivated by love and courageous enough to challenge the other person, then he must embrace that next responsibility of identifying the real behaviors that need to change. Because a change in the right behaviors will launch us toward growth. For example, in the case of Dave, my friend who struggled to read his Bible, it wasn't enough for me to simply tell him, "Just read it." The real behavior change he needed was to establish an increasing window of time in which he could read his Bible. And then as the window increased, I could push him to read with more maturity. Below is an example of a time-focused progression:

- **Weeks 1-10**: Set aside 10 minutes daily to read the Gospel of John.
- **Weeks 11-20**: Set aside 30 minutes daily to read 3 chapters of a New Testament book written by Paul.
- **Weeks 21-30**: Set aside 45 minutes daily to read an Old Testament book with Bible tools for deeper comprehension.

If Dave's problem was not a time issue but a comprehension issue, the behaviors would be different. I would ensure he was reading narrative books of the Bible that would give him a good overview, and have him read it with a Study Bible or something similar with commentary notes in the column. The example below takes Dave through John, which is a narrative on the life of Christ; Acts, which is a narrative of the church; and Genesis, which is a narrative of creation. All are easy to read and would give a novice reader a well-rounded understanding of the Bible. He could continue this pattern indefinitely until he read every page.

- **Weeks 1-5**: Read one chapter of the Gospel of John each day with a Study Bible, reading the text and then the companion study notes.
- **Weeks 6-10**: Read one chapter of Acts each day with a Study Bible, reading the text and then the companion study notes.
- **Weeks 11-20**: Read one chapter of Genesis each day with a Study Bible, reading the text and then the companion study notes.

While both of these reading plans might sound challenging, they provide an effective process for developing behavior patterns that support a goal of regularly reading the Bible or comprehending the Bible. Notice we are focusing on the behaviors—of time or comprehension—that support Bible-reading behaviors, and not just the vague goal of Bible reading. This type of rigid focus is critical in altering outcomes in our spiritual life. You must identify what I call the companion behaviors that will support the behaviors and goals you are trying to reach. This might require a little brainstorming with each other, but when done effectively it can become a tremendous tool for change in a man's life.

| MOTIVES | CHALLENGE | BEHAVIOR | CHECK-IN |

A leader's fourth responsibility is to check in. This requires a leader to ask the hard questions from meeting to meeting. Most of the time the hard questions entail the following: "What did you do?" and "Why or why not?" These are often the most annoying questions to answer because they force us to divulge our thoughts, actions, and attitudes, which reveal our motives. But this sort of transparency and vulnerability is essential to accountability. As a leader, you cannot lead a person into real change until you see his heart properly. The "What" question helps you to see the effort that your friend gave, and asking the "Why" question helps you to understand both his motives and how the two of you might adapt his behaviors for the next attempt. So learn your friend's motives; challenge him to modify the most relevant behavior; repeat until change happens. And remember, you will both be the leader at some point!

Next, let's look at the role of the participant. This role, while played by both men, is key to the speed of change. While change and growth are never fast, we can definitely work through our issues quicker when our goal is openness to change.

A participant has to
- **One** | Have an ownership mindset.
- **Two** | Willingly accept challenges.
- **Three** | Give up power with transparency.

First, you as a participant need to have an ownership mindset that kills the victim mindset. By this I mean that in your mind you are going to have to accept that your sins, issues, and behaviors are yours; they are not someone else's fault. This means accepting appropriate levels of responsibility for your thoughts, attitudes, and actions, and having a healthy understanding of God's sovereignty in regard to what He might be teaching you.

Unfortunately, all too often I have seen men caught in the victim mindset. They are typically very angry men who blame everyone else for their issues. They can be incessantly negative and see every other person's issues but their own. Some call this a form of blindness—a blind spot, or a dark side. But regardless of what you call it, understand that you can't move past the victim mindset until you claim ownership of your issues. Some men spend too much time blaming other people or events for the issues that arise in their life. This deflection is not conducive to change. Like boys who need to stop blaming their siblings for their own bad choices, we need to stop blaming our bosses, the stock market, our competitors, our government, and politicians for creating a suboptimal environment in which we've made poor decisions. To become a great man of God, you must set excuses aside and start owning your sins and addressing the things you can change.

Second, while in the participant role we need to welcome and embrace the opportunity to make a behavioral change. This means accepting the challenges your leader presents, making every effort to accomplish the goal. The leader can only be effective to the extent that you empower him, and a lack of submission here will severely reduce the speed of your spiritual growth. No leader wants to be in accountability with someone who never embraces a new challenge or never completes a task. Perhaps your leader will prove to be a very patient man, willing to listen to you complain about your shortcomings—but the accountability relationship won't become rewarding or fruitful until you become willing to listen to your leader's wise advice and commit to action. You've got to put some skin in the game.

In Resolute, our staff call these "hungry" men—men who are hungry for spiritual growth. We actively seek out these men and want them in our groups, because we know that their desire for growth will at times outpace our leadership. This dynamic produces unbelievable group and individual results. We understand that a man who favors change experiences the most favorable change. Therefore, want it, gentlemen!

Favor change and your change will be favorable.

The final requirement in this role as a participant is perhaps the most critical responsibility that either role must accept. You have to learn to give up. By "giving up" I mean that in this role you have to stop trying to conceal who you really are. Transparency is the key to successful accountability. Letting someone else put eyes on your failures and shortcomings is a game changer. You probably don't need the 80,000 pairs of eyes that Steve Young had on his field game, but you do need to let yourself be seen by the man sitting across from you. This requires you to actively choose transparency. When you become transparent about your issues, something incredible will happen in your accountability relationship: now your leader will know how to lead you.

I have seen this happen countless times in Resolute Cohorts during my time with those men. All it takes is one man to confess an ongoing hidden sin, one that he has been hiding for years, and in this moment of transparency the individual and the group experience a catalytic shift. This action of surrender results in rapid personal change, because it changes the dynamic of the relationship and the rules of engagement. When done right, and in confidential environments, this one event has the power to create an accountable relationship, the likes of which few men have ever experienced. Sometimes it can be overwhelming and hard to understand; most of us have never experienced accountability at this level, but when you taste of it, you will want more of it and you will become more authentic regarding the challenges and sins you face. It will cause you to drive deeper and further. And you know what you have done now? You have created a new field dynamic, establishing an environment of accountability.

Here is what happens as a result of giving up power through transparency:

- It changes the participant.It changes the environment or field dynamics of the relationship.
- It alters your leader's perception of you.It purifies your motivation through a humble and sacrificial act of taking a relational risk.
- It creates an expectation of accountability, because as soon as you go public, it makes the isue real, and behavioral change becomes an expectation.
- It creates an implicit assumption that both you and your leader are making a commitment to change.

RESOLUTE

When you meet each of the three participant requirements (adopting an ownership mentality, accepting behavioral challenges, and embracing vulnerability), you and your leader will be contributing equally to the accountability relationship. Doing your role well is important; it creates an environment of growth and change that will definitely pay off with rewards you have not experienced before in your spiritual life.

Last but Not Least: Complacency

Sometimes we notice negative behaviors creeping up in our lives; maybe we make an effort to change, maybe we figure we'll get to it later. But when these patterns become our new normal, this complacency can have serious destructive implications on our lives.

For example, our neighborhood has terrible internet and cell phone access—the very worst within the Twin Cities metropolitan area. When we walked into our potential new home for the first time, I noticed it immediately: the big "no service" text at the top left of the phone. Not even a single signal bar. We moved in anyway, and for eight years now this issue has plagued us. Our choices for internet service are limited to cable and dial-up. Easy choice, right? Well, we have five heavy internet surfers and cell phone users in the house who spend the day texting, making phone calls, watching movies and TV shows, and playing games. Each activity impacts our bandwidth, and often in the evening the cable internet service is crawling at dial-up speeds.

Everyone complains about it. We have been dealing with this issue for ages, because no, I do not want to call the internet provider. That would entail remaining on hold for long periods of time, waiting for a repair person to show up days later, ensuring that I am at home when they arrive in the middle of the work day, and then cutting a check. So we found a workaround: We simply reset the modem. This gives us smooth access for a period of time, right up until the next bottleneck. So we have adopted this new behavior where we reset the modem three times a day. And we have done this for months. Okay, maybe a year.

We have become so comfortable with this pattern that it is the new norm. It is just what we do. Since it "saves" time versus the whole process of calling the cable company, we have kept doing it.

Until recently.

My Wi-Fi network quit working, and I thought I was going to have a coup on my hands at home. The kids simply did not know what to do. Nobody to talk to, except each other. Imagine that! So I had to break the pattern and call the cable company.

It is incredible how fast the internet is when it works. In fact, we have been paying for very fast internet for years, but only began receiving the benefits last Friday.

Crazy, right? This is the choice of complacency.

Be careful before you judge me, because we all do this. We have unhealthy or destructive patterns that we embrace, cycling through over and over. These complacent areas of our life impede our spiritual growth; we are accustomed to the negative behavior, and we don't see enough benefit in addressing the matter to bother. Our urgency to address growth areas becomes non-existent. We fail to make spiritual progress. And so we become comfortable, entrenched. We barely notice the problem anymore, totally blind to the destruction it's causing. Remember: even if you don't desire accountability, you need it desperately!

Gentlemen, we are called to be accountable to each other. We cannot ignore this principle; it fills the pages of the Bible from cover to cover. So if you don't have another man in your life to be accountable to, your chances of failure are extremely high.

And men, there are so many advantages to accountability. Here are only a few:

- Encourages spiritual integrity.
- Increases our spiritual responsibility.
- Guards our spiritual freedom.
- Sharpens our spiritual gifts.
- Increases spiritual examination.

When accountability is successfully in play in a man's life, it will cause incredible positive impact. I have seen amazing results come out of even the first few timid steps forward. Accountability administered regularly in small doses can have a huge impact in so many areas of your life:

- Increased church engagement.
- Increased influence in the home.
- Increased love in relationship with your wife.
- Increased growth in faith.
- Increased spiritual disciplines.
- Increased spiritual awareness.
- Increased discernment in decision making.

And gentlemen, this is consistently true. If I hold another man accountable for a single thought, attitude, or behavior over the course of even one month, it has dramatic effects on his spiritual life and his motivations. I am not just talking about behavior modification, but deep life transformation; strict accountability leads to new outcomes that you may have been desperately struggling after for years.

Minor levels of accountability lead to change. This is not simple behavior modification, but genuine life transformation that in turn modifies behavior.

Use the Resolute System
HTTPS://BERESOLUTE.ORG/ACCOUNTABILITY

At the web address above, you will find everything you need to take this chapter further with your men's group:

- A printable Resolute Study Guide that supports this chapter.
- A weekly Accountability Report guide.
- Access to a Podcast and Video Curriculum.

Download the App for Your Men's Group

If you are looking for content to supplement your men's small group, we have extensive content for you. The Resolute Podcast App is a great tool, ready to go on your smartphone or tablet that will take the guesswork out of your next men's small group time. There is no extensive preparation needed; just walk into your men's small group, listen to the 15-minute podcast designed only for men, open the small-group discussion guide, and you have about 60 to 90 minutes of programming ready to go. This is great for mentoring or discipling other men, or if you are just looking for content for your men's group. We launch new and relevant men's material every quarter.

If you want more regular encouragement like this on your drive, you can also listen to our feeds on every major platform: iTunes, SoundCloud, Stitcher, and others; or just grab our feed right from the website.

REPENTANCE

Conviction requires us to understand what it really means to change—this is repentance.

My Story of Repentance

When I was just 20 years old, I experienced genuine repentance for the first time. I remember vividly the discovery of the spiritual power that flows out of repentance. It was a moment that prompted my decision to follow Christ.

But before we get to the moment of repentance, we've got to turn back the clock to when I was 15. My grandparents were the primary Christian influence in my life at that time, and on one particular Sunday morning, they made me go with them to church. Now, I just hated going to church, and had no expectation that anything interesting or meaningful was about to happen. Theirs was a small church, mostly attended by the "blue-hairs," as I called them. (When the bright white light hit the tops of the congregation's heads, the reasoning for that nickname became clear.)

On this particular Sunday, I was feeling a little down, as happens on occasion to a 15-year-old boy. And so I paid careful attention to the sermon, music, and readings, hoping to be surprised by something meaningful or comforting. The service was just as uneventful as usual—right up until the end of the sermon. The pastor then said that if you read the third chapter of Colossians every day for a month, it would change your life forever. He repeated his challenge again with stronger emphasis, and even threw a guarantee in there, saying, "I promise it will change your life forever."

So as a novice to this whole Christian thing, I decided to take God up on the challenge. And I have to say, I really believed in my head that God was going to do something—totally convinced. So I went home and found one of my grandparents' Bibles, smuggled it back to my room, and read it in secret for the next thirty days. I was faithful. Sometimes I read the chapter multiple times throughout the day, because I believed God was going to do something in my life.

Finally I came to the morning of Day 30. I woke up and read Colossians 3 again, and you will never guess what happened—nothing. That's right, nothing. Except I realized I had "accidentally" memorized the entire chapter. Interesting, right? So I just went on with life, thinking that although the Christian thing was nice for others, it did not seem to work for me. I liked some of the ideas, but I wasn't ready to make any sort of commitment.

Let's fast-forward to age 20. During that five-year jump, everything in my life had completely fallen apart. My relationships with my biological parents and friends had become poor to nonexistent; I dropped out of college twice, due to a lack of direction and commitment; I was partying with friends multiple days per week; work was nothing more than a way to keep the party funded.

My personal happiness had decayed into meaninglessness. I was beginning to realize that I had made a number of poor decisions that had created problems for me. I had hit what people often call "the bottom." I was alone and desperate for direction and purpose—with no idea how I might fill the void.

So after a night of partying with my so-called friends, I found myself back in my small apartment alone and deeply sad. This moment was the culmination of my despair. I climbed out of bed and approached the mirror over the sink only to look in and see this disfigured reflection of myself. It was as if I was looking into a funhouse mirror. I think my sight was affected from the drugs I had used the night before. I kept rubbing my eyes as I looked back into the mirror, but the image would not correct itself.

Suddenly this overwhelming emptiness and sadness came over me as I reflected on the decisions I'd made over the last few years. Who had I become? With deep unrest in my soul, I began to talk to the only person available—God. I asked Him one question, and I remember saying it out loud: "God, is this all life is about? I am willing to listen if You will just tell me." And suddenly it was as if God transported me five years into the past, and the words of Colossians came flooding back to me as God's audible answer.

If then you have been raised with Christ, seek the things that are above, where Christ is, seated at the right hand of God. Set your minds on things that are above, not on things that are on earth. For you have died, and your life is hidden with Christ in God. When Christ who is your life appears, then you also will appear with him in glory.

Put to death therefore what is earthly in you: sexual immorality, impurity, passion, evil desire, and covetousness, which is idolatry. On account of these the wrath of God is coming. In these you too once walked, when you were living in them. But now you must put them all away: anger, wrath, malice, slander, and obscene talk from your mouth. Do not lie to one another, seeing that you have put off the old self with its practices and have put on the new self, which is being renewed in knowledge after the image of its creator.

Here there is not Greek and Jew, circumcised and uncircumcised, barbarian, Scythian, slave, free; but Christ is all, and in all. Put on then, as God's chosen ones, holy and beloved, compassionate hearts, kindness, humility, meekness, and patience, bearing with one another and, if one has a complaint against another, forgiving each other; as the Lord has forgiven you, so you also must forgive.

And above all these put on love, which binds everything together in perfect harmony. And let the peace of Christ rule in your hearts, to which indeed you were called in one body. And be thankful. Let the word of Christ dwell in you richly, teaching and admonishing one another in all wisdom, singing psalms and hymns and spiritual songs, with thankfulness in your hearts to God.

And whatever you do, in word or deed, do everything in the name of the Lord Jesus, giving thanks to God the Father through him."
(Colossians 3:1–17)

For the first time, I had heard God speak to me. I know some will prefer to think of this not as an audible voice from God, but text memorized and recalled—but I experienced it then, and now, as a message directly from God to me, a response timed to perfection. There was no reason I should have recalled those words in that moment, yet I remember saying them out loud, an impulse I could not reject. With perfection I recited every word just as I had read it years before, and it was effortless. The words just came to me like a mandated call from the heavens.

I will never forget that encounter, and the spiritual and emotional clarity that followed. I realized that my life was not going in a direction I wanted. The only appropriate response was to make a change and head home to my grandparents, who had raised me from my teen years.

RESOLUTE

But the drive home was one of serious anguish. I had two hours of solitude to question the choice I had made. Would my grandparents accept me? Would they allow me to stay in their home? How would they view me, knowing the choices I had made? The incredible weight of my sin, the shame, and the consequences of my actions were irreconcilable in my mind. But there was nowhere else to go, and today I am thankful that there was wasn't, because the path to repentance was exactly where I needed to be.

As I pulled up to my grandparents' house, I knew I was about to make the most difficult walk of my life. It seemed not only hard, but impossible. I stopped my 1959 VW truck (yes, I know—cool, right?) in front of the house, where it sputtered silent. Looking up into the big picture window in the front of the house, I could see the two recliners that my grandparents relaxed in throughout the day. Both chairs faced the television with the chair backs to the window. My grandmother was not occupying hers but my grandfather was sitting in his. I could see him leaning back with his arms stretched out behind his shiny bald head. The moment I saw him, I felt so unholy in light of his faithfulness to both God and me. I was not sure if I could get out of the car, so I sat for a moment and tried to collect my strength. After a couple of minutes, I wiped the tears from my face, exited the truck, and began the walk toward the front of the house.

As I made my way, I noticed that my grandfather had vacated his chair. The front door opened, and he looked down at me from the top step. Before I could utter a word, he turned to my grandmother and said, "Grandma, our son has come home." (Years later I would discover this was a biblical reference to the story of the prodigal son, but I did not know or understand that in the moment.) My grandfather spread his arms wide, came to me, and embraced me with a long, warm hug, telling me he loved me and welcomed me in with no reservation. This was an incredible experience for me, and one of the major pivot points in my spiritual life.

Here I witnessed the grace, mercy, forgiveness, and love of God working though my grandfather. It was not the welcome I expected, but it was exactly what I needed. Within a few short months, my spiritual search for God and purpose would lead me to Jesus Christ. So the grace shown to me by my grandfather paved the way for an even more profound experience of grace with my Heavenly Father.

Repentance is the Core Message

Repentance is one of the great themes of the Bible, too prevalant to ignore. Yet repentance is not a popular message being proclaimed on platforms where the gospel is preached. It's a hard message, after all. Hard to hear, hard to apply.

But repentance is the core of the gospel message. It is an activity God requires, and one of the primary means through which He moves us from being convicted to living with conviction. We see, for example, that John the Baptist's entire ministry was built around the call to repentance.

"In those days John the Baptist came preaching in the wilderness of Judea, 'Repent, for the kingdom of heaven is at hand.'"

Matthew 3:1-2

It was also the main theme of Jesus' message when he launched His earthly ministry.

"From that time Jesus began to preach, saying, 'Repent, for the kingdom of heaven is at hand.'"

Matthew 4:17

Let's face it: repentance, at first glance, is not an easy matter. But if we are going to be men who "stand in the breach" we are going to have to address some challenging topics.

Men, it is not easy to do things like build a business, lose excess weight, raise teenage children, or train a young pet—and it is not easy to become a man who lives with conviction. It may seem impossible at times, and in fact may actually be impossible—unless we are willing to answer the call to repent. The process is difficult, but the payoff is worth every effort. Simply consider the present and eternal ramifications.

Repentance is Hard
So what makes repentance such a hard and heavy topic, one that the church often chooses to avoid presenting to the world? I see four basic reasons.

First, I think pastors worry about what people might infer from the very word "repentance." Some words mean different things to different people, and this is one such loaded word. There are at least two distinct theological understandings of what repentance is. And I can testify that it's difficult to communicate as a teacher if different factions in the audience are hearing fundamentally different messages. The tension of this theological debate boils down to two diametrically opposed statements. The first: "I repent, therefore Jesus saves." The second: "Jesus saves, therefore I repent." Both teachings are out there. So as a teacher, when I proclaim the need to repent, I have to wonder what my audience will infer. Will they think I'm telling them to plead for salvation? Or to respond appropriately to the salvation they've already received?

So as a teacher I have to take the time to push deeper, insisting that repentance is not some kind of tool that we can use to earn righteousness and salvation. Nothing in the entire Bible supports that definition. However, repentance involves activity and obedience, and because it does, it's easy to imagine, If I'm good enough, and I repent enough, then I will be in right standing with God. When exactly the opposite is true. Jesus initiates salvation, and in turn we live a repentant life.

The lack of clear understanding of what repentance means should encourage us to teach more, not less, on the topic. Jesus Christ Himself preached, "Repent, for the kingdom of heaven is at hand" (Matthew 4:17). If it was important enough for Jesus to communicate, we should probably go ahead and embrace this message too, and share it with others. We've just got to figure out how to live it out.

The second reason we don't like to talk about repentance is that it requires us to deal with pride. We men spend our whole life constructing this edifice of pride in our life. It's a false idol, fashioned in honor of the male ego. But this one word "repentance" requires us to address our entire value system. We must evaluate the beliefs we have collected over a lifetime. And when we examine our pride in light of the gospel, there can be no question: the edifice must be torn down. Which isn't an easy task. The male ego will fight to keep its power over you.

RESOLUTE

Thirdly, we avoid talking about repentance because we don't like the deep personal evaluation that repentance requires. Repentance is very, very, very personal. It requires me to admit that I was wrong for what I did. To admit that I've hurt somebody else. To admit that haven't just made a mistake—I've seriously offended God. And as a result, I have to do business with my emotions, feelings, and heart, only to find that I have to work up the courage and humility to reconcile with somebody else. Every part of this process is painful. And again, the male ego fights us every step of the way.

But the fourth reason we hesitate, and often the biggest reason, is that we simply don't understand what the word repentance means. So how does a person even go about repenting when we don't understand what it means? You have to admit, it is not a word we commonly use in our language.

So let's explore together. What does repentance mean? And how do I live out a life of repentance? If we can resolve these two questions, then not only will we understand repentance itself, but we'll see a path to greater conviction. I believe God has given us the tool of repentance to scrape away the callouses of our life. With fewer distractions and obstructions, we will be able to hear God's voice more clearly. And hearing more clearly, we will find it easier to respond.

Repentance Defined
So what does this cryptic word mean?

If you look inside the Bible, you'll discover that the word pops up over and over, especially in the Old Testament. You'll find over one hundred occurrences of the word in the New Testament, but over one thousand in the Old Testament.

Page by page, we find prophetic calls to repentance, along with stories of redemption flowing out of repentance, and cautionary tales of repentance refused.

And as we look at the word as it appears in Old Testament Hebrew, incredible meaning starts to take shape.

There are actually two different Hebrew words that have been translated into English as "repentance." The first, **naham**, means "to feel sorrow or regret." Repentance here is an emotional feeling for something that we've done to someone else; we regret the pain we have caused. The other Hebrew word is **shub**, which means "to turn, or to make an about-face in the opposite direction." So in this word we see that repentance includes behavioral change or action in addition to the feelings of regret. In other words, repentance means to feel sorrow and engage in a behavioral change.

Now this is a great definition, but to fully understand repentance, you have to see it in a real-life circumstance.

Repentance in Action

So let's look at Luke 15. Jesus tells three stories within this chapter, but I want to focus on the third. It's the story of the Prodigal Son. Now just so that we understand the context of the story, Jesus is telling a fictional story to illustrate a point. And He's going to illustrate the power of God's compassion towards us, describing God as a loving father, and us as the father's wayward children.

We see in the story a father's compassion towards his two sons. The younger son soon proves to be self-centered; the older, self-righteous. The younger brother's depiction draws out four qualities of genuine repentance. These qualities define, in Jesus' own words, what true repentance looks like in our own lives.

And Jesus said, "There was a man who had two sons. And the younger of them said to his father, 'Father, give me the share of my property that is coming to me.' And he divided his property between them."
(Luke 15:11-12)

The cultural implication of these words might go over our heads, but in a Jewish context, this would have been a shocking scenario. The younger son's request was the ultimate insult to a family patriarch. No Jewish son would have had the audacity to walk up to his living father and ask for his inheritance in advance. This would have been like saying, "I don't care about your values, your principles, your God, your property, or your future. Give me mine now, because I'm leaving." And surely no Jewish father would have granted such a request. A more acceptable cultural response by the father would have been, "Get out of the house. Take nothing with you. And get yourself a new last name, because you are no longer my son." But that's not what happens in the introduction to Jesus' story. Surely He had captured His audience's attention.

"Not many days later, the young son gathered up all he had, and took a journey into a far country. And there squandered his property in reckless living."
(Luke 15:13)

There's a decent chance that you have been in this place in life. And if so, you know the indignation and arrogance of this one moment. You probably even connect with the irrational blindness that insists, "I've got everything figured out, and I'm no longer going to listen to anybody else's opinion." When you've got all the answers, why not live life in whatever way you see fit? Well, if this line of thinking sounds familiar, the younger son might represent you as well as he represented me.

"And when he had spent everything, a severe famine arose in that country, and he began to be in need."
(Luke 15:14)

So not only did he waste the wealth his father gave him, but other circumstances arose that complicated his situation. Issues that were outside of his domain of control. And we learn that he didn't like the situation he had gotten himself into.

"So he went and hired himself out to one of the citizens of that country, who sent him into his field to feed pigs."
(Luke 15:15)

Now, for a Jewish man, this represented a grave violation of kosher law. Playing with swine was not an acceptable recreational activity. Nor was feeding swine an acceptable occupation. Yet Jesus put this younger son right in the pit with the pigs.

Just when you think it can't get worse...

"And he was longing to be fed with the pods that the pigs ate, and no one gave him anything."
(Luke 15:16)

So, have you ever been in this place?

Jesus is describing the darkest night of the soul. The lowest of human spiritual experiences. The bottom of life. This was as low as this Jewish boy could possibly go. And there was no way out. He was hungry, and no one cared. No one. And then right in the middle of this ugly mess, we see perhaps the most beautiful image of repentance in the Bible.

"But when he came to himself, he said, how many of my father's hired servants have more than enough bread, but I perish here with hunger. I will arise and go to my father and say to him, 'Father, I have sinned against heaven and before you. I am no longer worthy to be called your son. Treat me as one of your hired servants.' And he rose, and came to his father. But while he was still a long way off, his father saw him and felt compassion, and ran and embraced and kissed him."

(Luke 15:17-20)

This whole section is breathtaking, isn't it?

The image that Jesus paints is one of the father running toward his repentant son. Which is just an image of God running toward us. And from this short section of text, we can identify four qualities of genuine repentance. Four qualities that have the power to show us the way to conviction.

The Four Qualities of Repentance

Below are the four qualities of genuine repentance that Jesus describes in this story. You will notice we are adding two additional elements to our definition of repentance: the unseen qualities of awareness and motivation. According to Jesus' parable, repentance has four distinct qualities:

- **Mental awareness** of need for a change.
- **Emotional sorrow** over pain caused to others.
- **Changed action** from old behavior to new.
- **Sincere motivation** for the change.

The first quality of repentance is awareness. Luke 15:17 reads, "But when he came to himself..." Self-realization or awareness is the critical first step in repentance. It appears suddenly, but not randomly. We see that something specific had to trigger this rational process. The boy's father could not force the process of repentance upon him. But then something fired in the pistons of the son's mind, and it was a liberating moment for his understanding. His perspective on his entire life changed in an instant. This is spiritual awareness. And it's incredible when it happens, much like that time when Colossians 3 came back to me like a powerful flood. The mind itself begins to change. Let me illustrate.

Recently I had set a date with my wife for appetizers on a Friday night, which is a typical routine for us. On this particular occasion, my wife was meeting with a friend beforehand, so she was going to arrive a little later than normal. But in the spirit of being hungry, I decided to head to the agreed-upon restaurant at the usual time. Since I was by myself, I didn't want to take up a table, so I took a seat at the bar instead, and waited. Fifteen minutes stretched into twenty, into thirty, into forty. After waiting for nearly an hour, I began to wonder if my wife was ever going to come. So I sent her a text:

Hey, can I go ahead and order an app for us, 'cause I'm kinda hungry since it's 8pm. If I don't eat, I am going to die.

And she responded, Yeah, go ahead.

Now in the spirit of being happily married for twenty years, I decided to ask the all-important question:

Can I order any app I want?

We'd be sharing whatever I ordered, so it was important to give her chance to state a preference. Perhaps not sensing the gravity of the request, she responded, Yeah, go ahead.

And so I very quickly picked an item from the appetizer menu. It was called the Team Platter.

The bartender said, "Wow, I like your style."

I just sat there with a big grin on my face, happy to have impressed the man, even if I didn't really understand the comment.

About fifteen minutes later, one of the servers came out with an aluminum trash can lid. They had draped paper all over the inside of the lid with appetizers literally spilling out of it. Here is a full inventory of what the trash can lid couldn't quite contain: three pounds of french fries; ten chicken wings of various flavors; six cheeseburger sliders; two full-size chicken quesadillas; and a slab of steak cut into something called Bull Bites

As the server walked over, she made eye contact with me and saw that I was sitting alone. She then stopped to look around for the group who was supposed to receive the order.

And then she said, "Is this for you?"

"Oh no, that's not for me."

She looked up and down the bar again. "Are you sure this is not for you?"

"What's it called?"

She said, "This is the Team Platter."

"Oh," I said, "I guess that is for me."

She set the lid down on the bar. No kidding, it was so big, it hung off both sides of the bar.

"I'll be right back," she said. "I have to go get the sauces."

And so she brought back a separate plate containing a variety of ten dipping sauces. As she set this in front of me, I'm just looking down at this monster meal for an actual team, wondering how in the living world I am going to eat this. And right then, of course, my wife walked up to witness my ludicrous decision-making skills. Nice moment, right?

My wife looked down at the platter, then up at the bartender— back down at the platter—back up at the bartender—down at the platter—and finally she looked at me in bewilderment.

I didn't know what to say. I giggled in embarrassment, and then just started eating, engulfing myself in sauce and gluttony. I mean, I had to prove to the bartender that I was the man, right?

Later, as I was walking out of the restaurant, I had a moment of awareness as I reflected on my behavior.

This is Vince Miller. This is me. This is the mistake that I keep repeating in a variety of places of my life. I don't take the time to read carefully, and I fail to ask good questions when I don't understand.

Let me add that my failure to read and ask good questions is often followed by quick action. This can make for really good stories, but it doesn't make for very healthy experiences in my life. And so to protect me and those I love, over the course of my life, God has continued to bring this annoying weakness to my spiritual awareness in laughable ways.

What I have just illustrated in my own story is the very first step toward genuine repentance. Awareness leads us to repentance, which in turn moves us toward a life of conviction. This divinely inspired moment of self-discovery is critical, because here we learn that a particular ongoing behavior is liable to hurt ourselves and others. Very simply, we come to cognitive understanding that our actions are out of line with God's truth. In the story of the Prodigal Son, Jesus shows that the younger brother had a moment of cognitive awareness that was critical to his process of repentance. And notice it was awareness not only of his situation, but also of his own sin. This dialogue could only have happened between God and himself.

The Godly Sorrow of Repentance

The next quality of genuine repentance is godly sorrow. Here again is the younger son's confession:

"Father, I have sinned against heaven and before you."

I believe Jesus picked the words of this sentence carefully, and positioned them in a precise order. Notice how the son ranks the aggrieved parties: heaven first, and the father second. And notice that the son doesn't express sorrow for ruining his own life, or for wasting his father's wealth. His regret is not for the consequences of his sin, but for the sin itself. This distinction marks the difference between human regret and godly sorrow.

And men, it is very easy to diagnose the difference between these two. When a man comes to me to discuss a sin issue in his life, I can usually tell in the first five minutes which type of sorrow he is experiencing by the inflection in his voice, the phrases he uses, the way he talks about offended people, his present understanding of the situation, and the way he describes God. Sometimes it takes us a while to embrace godly sorrow when we are far from God's truth. But godly sorrow can be understood if we come to realize that the person we have offended most is God Himself.

Let me illustrate the difference so this principle will be crystal clear.

Eight years ago, my wife brought a Yorkie-poo home. The dog's name is Autumn, and she's a sweet little lap dog. My whole family loves this dog, but I've never taken to her. I am just not a pet guy. Call me crazy, but I believe animals belong outside.

So a few months ago, Autumn began leaving little "presents" all over the house. With each "present" my frustration and anger increased. Because of course I was left to deal with the mess from a pet I never wanted—a pet who was now soiling the carpet all over our home. A couple of times I became so angry with the dog that I told my wife, "If this does not get corrected I am going to have her put to sleep." And I will admit there were a few times where I completely lost my patience. In turn, my family was definitely frustrated with me—and had a right to be.

Then one day my wife finally agreed: "I think I should take her to the vet; her situation is not improving."
So my wife made the appointment—and then on the day of the visit, called me up to say, "Can you please take her? I have an appointment today, and if I take her, I am concerned I am going to be late."

And I said, "You do know how I feel about doing this, right?"

"Yes," she said. "But could you please do it?" I could almost feel her giving me puppy-dog eyes over the phone. And yes, she was literally begging. This was a rare moment for my wife.

I caved and responded, "Okay."

And then came one last awful instruction: "Don't forget the stool sample in the refrigerator!"

Yep, in our fridge. Where we keep the food that we eat. So now my head was spinning because dog doody was almost literally everywhere in my house—including the fridge!

But I calmed down and went home, and got the dog, the leash—and yes, the sample doody out of the fridge. Once at the clinic, I proceeded to explain what was going on, and the veterinarian did a little doggie physical. Then she took Autumn away to do some blood tests, and a few minutes later a nurse brought her back in. Shortly after, the doctor returned.

I could see on the vet's face that she had some bad news that she wanted to reveal as delicately as possible. She rested her arms on the tall exam table between us, hands folded, and sighed deeply. All the while I was just thinking to myself, Stop being so sensitive; bring it on.

At last she explained that Autumn had a serious case of Lyme's disease. A very inflamed form. Autumn was suffering from all kinds of complications. So the vet listed the treatment choices, then sighed again and said, "But if this doesn't work over the next thirty days, we're going to have to hospitalize Autumn for a few days."

Now, I'm not going to lie to you. This is exactly what was going through my mind: Ching, ching, ching, ching—all I heard was the sound of a cash register firing off expenses.

For about a minute, I could only think about how much this appointment was going to cost me. Do we have doggie health insurance? Is that even a real thing? If not, I should patent it.

And then as my mind slowed down, my thoughts turned to the suffering animal. Hold on a second. This is a really serious issue for Autumn. And I started to tune back in to the vet as she shared with me the details of Autumn's treatment. The severity of Autumn's illness became more pronounced to me as I went to pay for the visit. The nurse started loading up medicine in a bag and said, "We've never given so many medicines to a dog."

And I was thinking, You're a veterinary clinic, and you've never administered this much medicine for a sick pet? Suddenly something changed in my heart for Autumn. Me, a guy who is not a pet lover, who believes all animals should be outside, including hamsters—I started to experience a change of heart right then and there. I could feel my heart softening toward Autumn.

At home later that day, I had a conversation with the family. I explained the diagnosis, and we talked about how we could all help out with the thirty-day treatment. My heart change was reinforced by how the whole family responded—the children were especially heartbroken. Over the course of the conversation, my heart softened even further.

It took God about eight years, but I finally became concerned for our dog. To give you an idea of my heart change, in the week that followed, I actually took Autumn for a ride in the car, something I had never done with her before. Why? Because I felt something for her. Not human regret for myself because of the doody on the carpet, but sorrow for Autumn because of her illness. Isn't that interesting?

I think this is what God is hoping for from us. He's looking for a heart that is soft and sensitive to Him and others. Not self-pity, or sorrow over the consequences of our sin, but godly sorrow—a heart broken over the pain we have caused God's Son. And when our heart begins to soften, we are on the path to repentance.

The Action of Repentance

The third quality of genuine repentance is action. Notice what the young man said after becoming aware of his sin, and expressing godly sorrow for his actions:

"I will arise and go."

And so the younger son did something with his awareness and sorrow. Everything prior was internal, but it was time to act and demonstrate his repentant heart. Men, please hear me in this: this third step is critical to repentance and living with conviction. All kinds of great stuff can happen up in our head and in our heart, but if we don't do something in response, we're just being convicted, not acting on it. Once our words and deeds start to change, that's evidence that we're starting to live with conviction.

So this is your opportunity to tip the scales of life. You have to take a risk and act boldly. The next time God brings a sin to your attention and leads you through genuine godly sorrow, you have to take action to make things right. This is where the rubber meets the road.

Too often we do nothing and say nothing. We fail to act. Genesis 3:6 illustrates this perfectly, offering some of the saddest words for men in the Bible.

"Eve took of its fruit and ate, and she also gave some to her husband who was with her, and he ate."

This text depicts man at his worst. In the margins of the verse we can hear the echo of God's plea for a man to stand in the breach—yet Adam says nothing, and does nothing. Men struggle with many vices—pride, lust, envy, greed—but the greatest sin a man can commit is apathy toward God's instructions. When God has made it clear what we must do, we must act. Do not abdicate the leadership role God has given you to fulfill.

RESOLUTE

I love it when men act. I am not talking about aimless activity, but purposeful, God-centered action. The biblical stories about great men of faith—Noah, Abraham, Moses, Joshua, Nathan, David, Daniel, Peter, and Paul—these men and their stories inspire me, but only because they acted according to God's inspiration and call. So too can we. We men can stop sitting on the bench and get into the game. This is what I love about the younger son in Jesus' parable: his repentance doesn't end with a change in heart—he acts.

The Motivation of Repentance

REPENTANCE

| AWARE | SORROW | ACTION | MOTIVE |

The fourth quality of genuine repentance is sincere motivation. And this is the final and most important element. If we miss this, repentance is counterfeit. Awareness, sorrow, action— and sincerity of motivation. Notice the following comment by this young man; I believe it is one of the greatest sentences in the entire New Testament.

"I am no longer worthy to be called your son. Treat me as one of your hired servants."

We may not fully understand the potency of those words because of our cultural distance from Jewish life. But let's try to translate it to our cultural language: "I don't want my identity back at all. I don't need to be identified as your son. I will go without a name, and even my identity. I just want to be close to you again and under your care." And in an image of our heavenly Father, the father welcomed his son back with open arms. Much like my grandfather did for me.

One notable characteristic of the younger son's statement is how it contrasts with his brother's response:

"But [the older son] was angry and refused to go in. His father came out and entreated him, but he answered his father, 'Look, these many years I have served you, and I never disobeyed your command, yet you never gave me a young goat, that I might celebrate with my friends. But when this son of yours came, who has devoured your property with prostitutes, you killed the fattened calf for him!' And he said to him, 'Son, you are always with me, and all that is mine is yours. It was fitting to celebrate and be glad, for this your brother was dead, and is alive; he was lost, and is found.'" (Luke 15:28-32)

Do you want to see the true motivation of someone's heart? Refuse to reward the good things he has done, and do not punish the bad. Will he go on doing good, or howl at the injustice of the situation? What you have now is the exposed man.

When a man is not deeply convicted of sin, it is a pretty sure sign that he has not truly repented. Experience has taught me that men who have very slight conviction of sin sooner or later lapse back into their old life.

Dwight L. Moody

This is illustrated perfectly in the in the older son. Through his complaint, we learn that he believed his rewards for obedience were being taken from him upon the return of his younger brother. Thus he exposed his self-righteous jealousy. We notice at the end of the story that the older son was fixated on his own inheritance. His brother's return and reinstatement as a son threatened his future financial dividends—it had implications on his remaining inheritance. And so we see that a selfishly motivated self-righteous heart is only exposed when the reward is threatened. And what is the result of this impure motivation? The inability to come into the home to celebrate. The older son's joy was gone, because his joy was not based on the relationship with his father, but on the promise of the inheritance itself.

So we see that both sons had sinned and were in need of repentance, because neither son was motivated by love for his father. As the story ends, the self-centered son has repented and been welcomed back into the home. But the father's invitation to his self-righteous son lingers in the air.

Jesus has verified us for us the heart of true repentance. Genuine repentance declares, "Regardless of reward or punishment, I will do it—because it's the right thing to do."

What is truly shocking about this text is the application. Jesus compares two people in the text: a repentant sinner with an unrepentant Christian. Yep. And while it appears early in the story that the villain is the younger son, at the end we discover the older son stranded outside the party. Both were in need of repentance.

Did you catch that? This should be shocking for us as Christian men. Jesus leaves us hanging in a story that is yet to unfold our own lives. His teaching demands that the Christian man does some deep work in his heart to determine his motivation. Again: this should disturb us and make us uncomfortable.

Jesus is challenging us—men who are Christians. Jesus is asking us the ultimate question: What is your motivation? This question should deeply convict your heart and call you to live with conviction.

Bear fruit in keeping with repentance.

Matthew 3:8

God wants us to see in this story that the beauty of genuine repentance is that it leads to a life of conviction. He wants us to live in ongoing daily repentance so that we can discover the joy of living in relationship with Him. Repentance means becoming aware, and feeling true sorrow. It requires action and unselfish motivation. As we engage in the cycle of repentance, we deepen our relationship with Jesus Christ. And we become familiar with repentance as a tool to scrape away the callouses in our lives. As a tool to help us to feel again.

The Pain of the Process

I have a friend who formerly worked for the Minnesota Twins as a trainer. After practice he would occasionally bring a pitcher into the training room and, taking a very sharp scalpel, shave away the callouses on the pitcher's fingertips. The trainer would very gingerly shave away layers of calloused skin on the index finger, middle finger, and thumb. This is a common practice in baseball because callouses desensitize the nerves in the fingertips, causing pitchers to inadvertently grip the ball tighter and tighter. As the trainer scrapes away the callouses, nerve sensitivity returns so that the pitcher can feel the seams and apply pressure appropriately to the ball at the right location and time. For a seasoned pitcher to pitch correctly, he has to get the feeling back.

This trainer said that it was always interesting to get a fresh pitching recruit from the minor leagues and usher him into the training room for his first callous removal. These young pitchers had in many cases never seen this procedure before. They would often get extremely anxious and nervous, and for good reason—their hand is their most precious piece of equipment. It wasn't easy to entrust their fingertips to a trainer they had probably just met for the first time.

Gentlemen, we all fear the scalpel of repentance in our life. There will be pain, exposure of callouses, feelings of shame and regret, and a need to seek forgiveness. But on the other hand, do you really want to go on through life feeling convicted? Or are you ready to live with real conviction?

Perhaps in these moments of pain, God is trying to tell us something. Maybe He is trying to get our attention and move us onto the path of genuine repentance. Maybe God is trying to peel away the layers of our calloused life, using repentance as a tool to restore feeling. And I believe when we engage in it—not just one time, but on a daily basis—God uses this tool to deepen and enrichen our devotion to Him.

If my people who are called by my name humble themselves, and pray and seek my face and turn from their wicked ways, then I will hear from heaven and will forgive their sin and heal their land.

2 Chronicles 7:14

Use the Resolute System

HTTPS://BERESOLUTE.ORG/REPENTANCE

At the web address above you will find everything you need to take this chapter further with your men's group. Just like in the last chapter you will find the following resources:

- A printable Resolute Small Group Guide that supports this chapter.
- Access to an Audio Podcast and Video Curriculum that gives you ready-made video content for your men's group.

DESIRES AND REPETITIVE SIN

Living with conviction means delivering a fatal blow to the ultimate enemy of conviction —ungodly desires that lead to repetitive sin.

I count him braver who overcomes his desires than him who conquers his enemies; for the hardest victory is over self.

Aristotle

"And I sought for a man among them who should build up the wall and stand in the breach before me for the land, that I should not destroy it, but I found none" (Ezekiel 22:30).

I have to tell you, these words, they drive me crazy. They make me want to jump out of my seat. They make me want to throw my hand in the air and shout, "Here am I, send me."

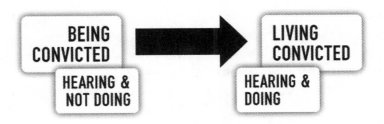

And I want you to respond the same way. What we're trying to figure out is how we can move from being convicted—wishing we could answer God's call—to actually living our life with conviction. There's a cavernous distance between those two ends of the spectrum. And I believe that God wants us to be men who will stand in the breach on His behalf.

We began this book by saying there were four factors that could help us. The first one was accountability, even tiny amounts of which will propel conviction farther than you anticipate. Yes, just tiny amounts. I suggested that accountability requires both a willingness to be held accountable, and an environment conducive to accountability. We have to step into accountability now. Because that tiny little bit of accountability will drive your convictions farther, pushing you toward a true life of conviction.

In the last chapter we discussed repentance. We said that repentance is a tool that helps us understand our relationship with Christ. And we identified four qualities of genuine repentance: awareness, sorrow, action, and sincere motivation of the heart. Repentance is not a tool through which we earn salvation or righteousness with God, but a means to go deeper with God. Because we love God, we are driven to take action and walk away from the behaviors that damage our relationship with Him.

And here we will look at the third factor that affects our ability to live with conviction: desires that lead to repetitive sin.

If you are a Christian man, regardless of how long you've been in a relationship with Christ—if it has been for just a few hours, or for a lifetime—you are in the business of tackling sin. This endeavor is a key part of every Christian man's journey. And so, just for a few moments, what I'd like to have you do is think of a sin in your life. Just think of one sin, not all of them.

RESOLUTE

Perhaps there is one sin that you have lived with for a long time. Let's call it a repetitive sin. So I want you to think about that right now. And I don't want you to think about your wife's, or your neighbor's, or your children's sin. Just think of yours.

_____

Write it here:

_____

Now I want you to think about the mental dialogue that you go through as you face this sin. It probably goes something like this.

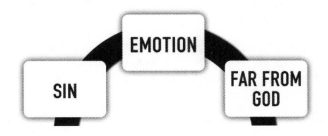

First you sin, then you feel a range of emotions, and finally you feel further from God than before. Then you do it again—you sin, you feel shame, and you feel the distance growing.

You sin again, and now you feel unforgivable.

You sin again, and figure out a justification for the behavior. Maybe you don't even need forgiveness after all. Which means you don't need to talk to God about it. Maybe you're distant, but it's a safe distance.

If you know what I'm talking about, then you know the power of this pattern of defeat. You've felt the psychological power of repetitive sin. And as you're thinking about this cycle, I want you to hear this: if you are desperate to defeat repetitive sin in your life, then you are reading the right chapter at the right time. Because in this chapter we're going to deliver a mighty blow to repetitive sin in your life forever.

Gentlemen, we are going to deal with this sin, and it's going to be epic. Because there is nothing that's a greater conviction killer than the cycle of repetitive sin. Nothing does more to keep us stuck mentally and emotionally, stunted in our spiritual growth, and stagnant in our relationship with God. So let's go kill the pattern that seems to be killing us.

"Today, the greatest challenge facing American evangelicals is not persecution from the world, but seduction by the world."

C.J. Mahaney

Desire and Repetitive Sin

Let's imagine your favorite meal for a moment. Or better yet, let's imagine mine.

My favorite meal is a young and tender 8-ounce filet minion. The month-long curing process has made it soft and flavorful. It has been heated to medium-rare and then peppercorn crusted. Warm and dripping with flavor in the middle, it is nice and charred on the outside. The steak is served warm with a fresh pat of real butter on top that is dripping down the sides. As a side, fluffy twice-baked potatoes with butter, salt, and pepper. And last, crispy steamed and seasoned asparagus. Oh, I love this meal. I am hungry just describing it.

Hopefully you are hungry right now too. And there is a reason why you "feel" a little hungry. In just reading this description, the hypothalamic gland in your brain sent out appetite-stimulating neurons to the rest of your brain and thus told you something like, "That sounds wonderful!" Unless there was something in the meal you personally don't prefer—maybe you are vegan, and only the vegetables sounded nice. But for me, this is my perfect meal. And there is nothing like the stimulation of eating the meal I described above.

Occasionally the meal-eating experience is so desirable and pleasurable, we reinforce this by overeating. We cannot seem to stop eating because the stimulation is so incredible. Sometimes the stimulation is reinforced by environmental factors, such as descriptive terminology on a menu, social pressure from our relatives at Thanksgiving, cultural customs that encourage overeating, or large helpings at restaurants that serve Team Platters! And sometimes, before you know it, your desires have you. You have overeaten. First overstimulated, now you are overstuffed.

This is a perfect example of out-of-control desires. I believe we too often let many of our desires control us, especially in American culture where we can have everything on the spot. Many of us live completely "out-of-control," or rather completely controlled by our own desires. Often we give no consideration to our desires; we let them lead us and rarely consider that they may be out of line with God's desires for us. Rather than lead our desires in a Godly direction, we often submit to them and let the hypothalamic glands of our spiritual life rule over our outcomes.

The big question of this chapter is, Do we have a deep abiding hunger for God in our spiritual life? Or are we so overstuffed with material things that we have no space for God?

Our Desire Problem

With this in mind, let's look at the out-of-control life that follows when our desires are in control. Repetitive sin is ultimately a desire problem. So if we can understand desire, then we can successfully attack repetitive sin. Here is the Apostle Paul's perspective:

But I say, walk by the Spirit, and you will not gratify the desires of the flesh. For the desires of the flesh are against the Spirit, and the desires of the Spirit are against the flesh, for these are opposed to each other, to keep you from doing the things you want to do. But if you are led by the Spirit, you are not under the law.

Now the works of the flesh are evident: sexual immorality, impurity, sensuality, idolatry, sorcery, enmity, strife, jealousy, fits of anger, rivalries, dissensions, divisions, envy, drunkenness, orgies, and things like these. I warn you, as I warned you before, that those who do such things will not inherit the kingdom of God. But the fruit of the Spirit is love, joy, peace, patience, kindness, goodness, faithfulness, gentleness, self-control; against such things there is no law.

And those who belong to Christ Jesus have crucified the flesh with its passions and desires. If we live by the Spirit, let us also keep in step with the Spirit. Let us not become conceited, provoking one another, envying one another.
(Galatians 5:16-26)

These are amazing words from Paul, and within them is the secret to defeating repetitive sin in our life. I want to make four observations about this particular text. First: there's a war being waged inside of me, and inside of you. Again, the battle is internal. I am not engaging an outside force, but within my mind, soul, and spirit, my flesh and the Spirit of God battle for control. The internal nature of this war does not diminish the reality of its existence or the importance of its outcome. We as redeemed people live in two states—flesh and spirit. And these competing natures are forever at war within us.

I like to call this "spiritual cognitive dissonance." Now what is cognitive dissonance? The simultaneous belief of two contradictory ideas, or the attempt to explain away a piece of data that contradicts a firmly held belief. For instance, I might think to myself, I'm still on a diet, while stuffing a doughnut into my mouth. Okay, so I've actually done this. I've eaten a doughnut—all 250 deep-fried, chocolate-covered calories—while promising myself that I could cancel it out by adding a mile to my run. Perhaps you've allowed yourself similar cheats. Well, I hate to disappoint you, but I've looked it up, and nutritionally this doesn't actually work.

I believe that Christians live in a spiritual form of cognitive dissonance. And I believe that Paul confirms that spiritual cognitive dissonance is a real thing. In the above passage from Galatians 5 he alludes to it, but in Romans 7, his teaching is explicit.

For we know that the law is spiritual, but I am of the flesh, sold under sin. For I do not understand my own actions. For I do not do what I want, but I do the very thing I hate. Now if I do what I do not want, I agree with the law, that it is good. So now it is no longer I who do it, but sin that dwells within me. For I know that nothing good dwells in me, that is, in my flesh. For I have the desire to do what is right, but not the ability to carry it out. For I do not do the good I want, but the evil I do not want is what I keep on doing. Now if I do what I do not want, it is no longer I who do it, but sin that dwells within me. (Romans 7:14–20)

Now that is the greatest tongue twister in the Bible, but it explains exactly how I feel regarding repetitive sin. I do what I don't want to do. And the thing that I want to do, I fail to do. Have you ever experienced this? Well, if you've lived with repetitive sin, then yes, you have. So have I.

But let's make another key observation in Galatians 5—Paul offers us a simple way to determine whether we're being controlled by our flesh or God's Spirit.

Notice the two rather long lists of outputs. If you are an engineer, you probably already identified these in your first reading. Paul begins with a disturbing list of negative outputs: "Sexual immorality, impurity, sensuality, idolatry, sorcery, enmity, strife, jealousy, fits of anger, rivalries, dissensions, divisions, envy, drunkenness, orgies, and things like these." And then there's this nice short list of positive outputs: "Love, joy, peace, patience, kindness, goodness, faithfulness, gentleness, self-control; against such things there is no law." One list is what our flesh produces, the other is the fruit of God's Spirit at work in us.

The third teaching to note is that God rewards our output, whether godly or sinful. The reward for repetitive sinful behavior is that we get to live in a prison of our sin. We call this slavery to sin. I know this doesn't sound like a fun reward, but it's what we've earned in this instance. In Romans 1:24 Paul says, "Therefore God gave them up in the lusts of their hearts to impurity, to the dishonoring of their bodies among themselves." Now how about that for a reward? If you are a process thinker, then you have probably already concluded that the rewards of flesh-controlled living are not all that appealing.

On the other hand, you've got this positive list of outputs with a different kind of reward. This reward is a life of freedom. Now that sounds really good. And that's where Paul wants us to live—in the freedom of the Spirit.

So in the midst of these conflicting processes of outputs and rewards, let's pull back and make our fourth observation—and this one is critical. The key to defeating repetitive sin is selecting the right input to ignite the best process. And what is the input? The input is desire.

Notice what Paul says in Galatians 5:16-17.

"But I say, walk by the Spirit, and you will not gratify the desires of the flesh. For the desires of the flesh are against the Spirit, and the desires of the Spirit are against the flesh, for these are opposed to each other, to keep you from doing the things you want to do."

It's all about our desires. And that one word right there is the key to us understanding how we can defeat repetitive sin in our life. Let's dig into this word desire.

Defining our Desires

Desire is a fantastic word. I've studied this word for a number of years, and it is a word in the ancient New Testament Greek that explodes with meaning. The richness of this word just makes my head spin. In Greek, the word indicating desire is epithumeó. This Greek word can be used as a noun, indicating motivation or longing or commitment—or it can be a verb, meaning to covet or to lust after something or someone. The word is also unique because it references something happening inside of us that drives the behaviors (outputs) of our life. The word contains two compound root words that clarify its meaning. Epi ("focused on") and thymos ("passion or lust"). So its simplest definition is "a focus on passion." With this meaning in mind, reread Galatians 5 and see how the passage comes to life.

Below you see a matrix of possibilities that can occur with our desires. I like to call it the Desire-Motivation Matrix. And Paul is going to lay it out so beautifully for us.

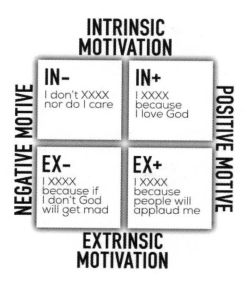

Because desire is multi-dimensional, it is valuable to matrix the concept, as we see in the Johari window above. Desire can have outputs that are both positive (right column) and negative (left column) as Paul describes. The type of output, remember, is based on the nature of a person's motives or desires. And so Paul clarifies that we are internally motivated by the Spirit (top row), or externally motivated by the flesh (bottom row).

RESOLUTE

Now let's watch this play out in our Johari window. Internal negative is the first box on the upper left-hand corner. Then drop down to external negative, then external positive, and finally internal positive. We'll walk through an application of this matrix as it relates to a spiritual discipline, and then we will find a better understanding of how desire works.

The concept I want to drop into the matrix is giving. Most Christians understand that giving is a form of worship, a discipline, and something that God commands us to do. But have you ever considered the motivation behind it? So let's drop the word "give" into the blank lines within the windows of the matrix. In the Internal Negative window, we read, "I don't give, and I don't care to give." So here is a very resistant heart—an unwilling heart acting (or remaining inactive) through negative motivation.

Shift down a window, and you come to External Negative. "I give, because if I don't, God will punish me or withhold blessing." Such a person is motivated by the fear of divine judgment. And there are many who teach this theology and reinforce it with partial truths taken from their life experiences.

Now watch as our desire matures even more. Let's move one window to the right, into the positive side of motivations and desires. Within the External Positive window, the heart says, "I give, because other people will applaud me." A person with this motivation does good things out of a desire for recognition. And we all understand this type of motivation. From when we were children, we have been taught that if you do something correctly you will be rewarded. In adulthood this type of motivation is still reinforced by applause, awards, incentives, and bonuses. Using our example, give generously enough and you might get your name on a building, or maybe gain influence in a process or leverage over people. So the good works are extrinsically motivated.

Finally, we come to the Internal Positive window. And here we experience the true joy of giving. Within this window we find the deepest of desires and the purest motivation: "I give because I love God."

Now look back at this Johari window and notice how our desires changed as we moved from corner to corner. Do you see the progressive movement toward spiritual maturity? Perhaps you, like me, have spent time in each of these stages as you've learned the discipline of generosity. Or perhaps now you see an opportunity for growth.

But let's drop something a little bit more fun into the matrix. Something a little closer to home, but easier to talk about.

I share a house with multiple teenagers, and I have learned that tidiness is a struggle for my kids. They are capable of cleaning their room, but their desire isn't quite as mature as it could be. So on their behalf, let's drop this issue into the matrix.

- **Internal Negative Motivation:** I'm not going to clean my room, nor will I ever clean my room.
- **External Negative Motivation:** I'm cleaning my room, because if I don't I will be punished.
- **External Positive Motivation:** I'm cleaning my room now, because my friends are coming over, and I don't want to look like a pig.
- **Internal Positive Motivation:** I'm cleaning my room, because I want to.

Oh, to see the day when we finally get to that last window of the matrix. The day when I don't have to pester my teenagers to clean their rooms, because they've already done it on their own initiative. Maybe someday, but definitely not today.

By now you should understand how the matrix works. We all go through a maturation process of our desires and motivation. And I believe Paul in Galatians 5 is hoping that we will embrace this process. Here he paints a picture of what pure internal motivation looks like—where we are led by the Spirit and focused on our love for God—and the icing on the cake is all the positive outputs and rewards that follow. We don't act godly for the fruit—the fruit is simply produce, output from the process. Paul is giving us a target to aim for, stating clearly that we can identify our desires, mature them, and direct them toward godly objectives, outcomes, and rewards.

Armed with the concept of maturation, we now can learn how to deliver a mighty blow to repetitive sin. Because killing repetitive sin is all about attacking sin at the desire level.

Steps to Defeating Repetitive Sin

Ready to go on the offensive? Here are four steps to defeating repetitive sin in your life; after I explain them, I'm going to illustrate for you how I use them in my own life.

First, if you want to defeat repetitive sin in your life, and live life with conviction, you have to consciously decide that you're done with your sin of _____ .
(Go ahead and fill in the blank.) You have to consciously decide in your heart and mind that you will no longer be beaten down by this sin that just keeps manifesting itself in your life. Make the all-important decision that Satan has beaten you down long enough; declare war against this sin and the core issue. Starting immediately you're going to consciously do something about it. And when you make this conscious decision while applying the teachings covered in the previous two chapters, you will discover a powerful breakthrough. When you declare war against your sin, establish accountability, and strive toward repentance, then you will see real change in your life.

Remember, it isn't enough to simply say, "I'm done with this sin." A quiet statement of good intentions can amount to nothing but a smokescreen—we can deceive ourselves into thinking we'll deal with a problem, when the truth is we aren't taking any of the necessary steps. But when you make the same statement to an accountability partner, he is going to dig out the core issues with you. So within an environment of accountability, and with a repentant heart, you deliver a fatal blow to the grip of repetitive sin when you speak out against it. Because now it is no longer unchecked, and you are no longer facing it alone.

The second step toward defeating repetitive sin is to describe and identify some things. Now this is of utmost importance. With an accountability partner beside you and a notepad in front of you, you need to describe in detail what happens every time you deal with this repetitive sin. What is going on with you physically, emotionally, and environmentally at the time you commit this sin? And yes, in detail.

Now there are some of you who experience a repetitive sin in a variety of environments. If this is your case, then you need to look for the commonalities and describe them in as much detail as possible.

I want you to identify two things as you're describing this sin. You're looking for a trigger, and you're looking for a reward. Both the trigger of the sin, and a reward for the sin.

One of the reasons we repeat sin again and again is because we are being rewarded for it. There are very powerful, short-lived rewards that accompany your sin. They are often intoxicating. In fact, sometimes they're so powerful that people become psychologically dependent to the cycle of the sin. So no matter what, you've got to find the trigger and the reward that keeps you coming back for more. You have to write it down and you have to understand it.

The third step is to make an advance decision on what you're going to do next time you get into the situation that triggers your sin. You will need to be ready to act before you can be tempted by the reward of your sin. An advance decision is crucial because it helps to separate the trigger from the reward. It also aids in taking the guesswork out of what you should do when the trigger strikes. So you're going to choose today what you will do then. It doesn't need to be a complex decision—just a simple one will help you respond to the trigger without considering the reward, and thus stop the cycle.

An advance decision is crucial because it helps to separate the trigger from the reward.

Here is an example of a simple advance decision: "The next time my trigger strikes, yet before I act on this sin, I'm going to remove myself from _____ environment." This conscious advance decision keeps you from reasoning toward the bad reward and bends your corrupt thinking and behavior toward a God-honoring reward. Make sure you write your strategy down and share it with your accountability partner; this will ensure you have the necessary support in place when the trigger strikes.

The fourth and final step is to attach a godly reward to the problematic desire. So you're going to remove the bad reward, and you're going to focus your heart on something more beautiful. You cannot simply turn desires off, because we are created to desire. You must show your desire a reward that is actually worth pursuing. And this object of godly desire? God Himself. It is God whom we can pursue through the supernatural power of the Spirit. And when we desire Him we can expect two things: a battle with sin, and the endless rewards of the fruit of the Spirit.

These four simple steps require a little bit of thinking and a whole lot of accountability, but are powerful enough to break a corrupt belief system and reorient our desires.

My Repetitive Sin

Now let me show you how this four-step process plays out in my life.

My repetitive sin is my need to control. Most people would never know this about me since I appear laid back and in most situations I am very easy-going. To outsiders, I appear calm, but the truth is I struggle with deep levels of anxiety. I typically wake at 2:00 AM and usually cannot fall back to sleep because my mind is processing all the situations, issues, and concerns of my everyday life. This pattern has impacted my sleep patterns since I was a teenager and thus I have learned to live on very little sleep.

Unfortunately, when my anxiety rises to a heightened level, it spurts out toward others. And the people closest to me experience the harshest consequences of my anxiety. Little spurts of anxiety here and there are often manifested as frustration, impatience, detachment, or short-temperedness.

So a few years back, I had a moment where I made a conscious decision—step one in the process of killing repetitive sin. My resolution was this: "I am going to deal with my anxiety because it is affecting the people closest to me."

In taking step two, I had to identify and describe the triggers and rewards. So here's typically what happens inside of me: I start to make commitments, and because I believe that I can do anything, I commit to do too much. Here is what literally comes out of my mouth: "Yeah, I'll do that. Yeah, I'll do that. Yeah, I'll do that. Yeah, I'll do that." And because I want to do everything with excellence, I start exerting energy, time, and effort into every activity. Pretty soon the activities I have committed to are absorbing my life and engrossing my mind. And as these activities begin to consume me, I get lured in by my own need to control the process and the outcome. When it continues for too long, then I start losing patience. Everyday issues—and the people attached—all begin to feel like obstacles to productivity.

My trigger, then, is the loss of control. I have a strong desire to control the outcomes of all activities, and this desire to control drives me narrow my focus and work harder without considering the needs and feelings of those around me. And what is the reward? Well, the reward is when someone says to me, "Vince, great job," or "Vince, you nailed it!" I know you know what I'm talking about. This one is especially rewarding: "Wow, that was incredible." Oh, that one is a killer for me, a very compelling reward.

With my trigger and reward identified, I need to make an advance decision. What will I do next time I wake up at 2:00 AM, overwhelmed by unneeded anxiety? This is my strategy: Instead of letting my desires control me, I just get out of my bed and get down on the floor, and I start praying. I started doing this a few years ago and it has been the greatest anxiety reliever of my life. I also decided to make an advance decision about the number of commitments I make, and the way I consider the proposal. Whenever possible I evaluate, pray, and get counsel before giving a decision. And I've got to tell you, these advance decisions have helped to significantly lower my anxiety and improve how I respond to the people closest to me.

What has been powerful is that God has shown me that my anxiety not only has the power to drive me away from God and other people, but it also has the potential to drive me toward God and others. Whenever my anxiety is starting to well up, I turn to prayer, and this time of conversation usually drives my anxiety away and turns my desires away from the cares of the world and toward God instead. It turns a negative internal motivation into a positive internal motivation and desire. In my anxious prayers I discover I have the opportunity to "cast my cares upon him" (1 Peter 5:7), and in doing this I have leveraged an old trigger and repurposed it. Since God commands me to surrender my anxieties, cares, and concerns to Him, I can push the focus of my heart from the work at hand to the God I serve, until I finally come to embrace the correct perspective: "God is big enough to handle it, so why not let Him handle it."

Which leads me to the last step: attaching a new reward to the desire. And my new reward is peace—a peace that comes from a new focus on the sovereign God who can handle my problems or issues even if I have created the issues myself. He can work through every one of the problems that I am trying to control. These include the issues I am trying to power through or strategize through on my own. And when God handles them, I get divine rewards and human rewards. Which means it is no longer, "Wow, great job, Vince"—it's "Praise to our awesome God." And God's rewards are far more incredible.

Hopefully you see the difference in the power of this reward. Now I am doing battle with a supernatural event that is happening in me, while simultaneously delivering an incredible blow to repetitive sin. And you know what? Anxiety, over the last few years, has become my best friend. I am sure I will always live with this as my "thorn in the flesh," but I praise God for my thorn because it continues to drive me toward Him.

Wow, think about that. I have turned what was formerly a defeating and repetitive sin into what is now my power unto godliness. And I would never again ask God to take this sin from me because it is what drives me to His feet daily. I enjoy delivering a blow to Satan on a regular basis, through a trigger that used to defeat me. Now this trigger leads to a godly response, and my reward is that I can live in step with the Spirit. I am no longer living in a prison of my own anxiety. Isn't that great stuff?

No matter what your repetitive sin may be, when you defeat it, the reward is freedom. Freedom in Christ.

Desire God, not Sin

Gentlemen, you can wage war with your repetitive sin. Make sure that you don't depend on your own strength; it is the Holy Spirit in you that will win the fight. You must follow and keep in step with the Spirit. Then the Spirit takes hold, and God is glorified.

You know what I've learned about desires in my journey of trying to understand my own? God wants us to desire. He wants you to desire. We don't have a desire problem; our problem is that we focus our desires on the wrong objects.

Back at the beginning of the Bible, in the very first chapters of Genesis, God created us with longing in our hearts. We often miss that fact because we're so tantalized by the creation of light, the planet, and man. But what's interesting about God's order of creation is that when He created man, He left man with what appeared to be a deficit. He created man and populated the earth with everything except another human being. But it only appeared to be deficit; as we know, God never does anything by accident, and this was no accident. God created man without woman, and then He waited. Inside of man, God was stirring man's desire. He was allowing it to smolder and build until man become conscious of his desire for something more—until man recognized the need for another human relationship. And then finally God fulfilled that desire within man. God became the means for fulfilling man's desire, and taught him a lesson we have to learn time and time again: our desires are best fulfilled through our Creator and not His creation. Of course we know that Adam messes this all up in the very next chapter, following his own desires. And as a result we have been stuck in this internal war ever since. We are still learning the tough lessons about finding the fulfilment of our desires in God alone.

Men, let's desire God and allow Him to fulfill the desires of our heart. In turn He will lead us toward a greater understanding of what it means to not just be convicted, but to live with deep conviction.

Use the Resolute System

HTTPS://BERESOLUTE.ORG/REPETITIVE-SIN

Just like in the last chapter you will find at this web address the following resources:

- A printable Resolute Small Group Guide that supports this chapter.
- Access to an Audio Podcast and Video Curriculum that gives you ready-made content for your men's group.

COMMITMENT

Living with conviction means understanding the full commitment of being a disciple: identity formation combined with ongoing self-denial.

"And I sought for a man among them who should build up the wall and stand in the breach before me for the land, that I should not destroy it, but I found none."

Ezekiel 22:30

As I said at the beginning of this book, I think the challenge to "stand in the breach" is intended to be motivational. God is trying to motivate you and me to get off the bench and into the game. He's looking for men who will stand in the breach. Men who will do something with their life—who will live with conviction and not simply be convicted. And my aim throughout this book has been to echo God's call and show you how to respond. My prayer is that you have felt challenged and are even now making steps to get into the game of life as a follower of Christ.

I suggested four factors would move us from being convicted to living with conviction. We've already looked at accountability, genuine repentance, and God-focused desire. The fourth factor to explore is the commitment of a disciple.

In this chapter we are going to dive into Luke 14, and I want to show you an interaction between Jesus and a large crowd of His followers. Out of this story we will learn the two requirements of true discipleship under Jesus Christ.

I will warn you that this will be the most difficult chapter to apply, because it is a difficult message. But it is not my message—Jesus Himself gave this teaching. If we're going to understand what it means to truly live our life with conviction, then we have got to understand the base requirements that God has established for a disciple, a follower, a Christian man. Without this understanding, we can't understand how to follow Jesus Christ, becoming an adherent of His way. So let's take a look.

The Overwhelming Call to Discipleship

Now great crowds accompanied him, and he turned and said to them, "If anyone comes to me and does not hate his own father and mother and wife and children and brothers and sisters, yes, and even his own life, he cannot be my disciple. Whoever does not bear his own cross and come after me cannot be my disciple.

"For which of you, desiring to build a tower, does not first sit down and count the cost, whether he has enough to complete it? Otherwise, when he has laid a foundation and is not able to finish, all who see it begin to mock him, saying, 'This man began to build and was not able to finish.' Or what king, going out to encounter another king in war, will not sit down first and deliberate whether he is able with ten thousand to meet him who comes against him with twenty thousand? And if not, while the other is yet a great way off, he sends a delegation and asks for terms of peace.

"So therefore, any one of you who does not renounce all that he has cannot be my disciple. Salt is good, but if salt has lost its taste, how shall its saltiness be restored? It is of no use either for the soil or for the manure pile. It is thrown away. He who has ears to hear, let him hear."

(Luke 14:25–35)

Let me ask you a question. Have you ever engaged in a project where, after you started it, you realized you bit off more than you could chew? I'm sure we've all been there. Now I want you to recall what that overwhelming moment feels like.

Twenty years ago, I got into a project that was more than I can chew: I married an interior designer. And I didn't realize that when you marry an interior designer, for the rest of your waking life you are destined to become by default a general contractor. That's basically been my job for the last twenty years of marriage. And yes, I have found every creative way possible to decline all the "little projects" that my wife suggests that I do. It takes a little craftiness, but I have worked every angle known to man.

Last year, no kidding, this happened: I decided to put a new thermostat in my home, because I was tired of my wife saying to me in bed, "Would you go turn up (or turn down) the thermostat?" So I took our old model off the wall, and I upgraded to a new sleek Wi-Fi–enabled model—the nicest product I could find. This new unit was much smaller than the old thermostat, and so I could see traces of the wall's previous paint job. There were even a few gaps in the wall I'd have to spackle over—but nothing I couldn't handle. After I was done with the installation, I went to my wife and said, "Hey, look at the sweet new thermostat that I put in." And she walked over, looked at the thermostat for maybe a second, and immediately pointed out the holes in the wall and the exposed paint.

"What is this?" she asked. I explained that the new unit was a little smaller, but those little cosmetic issues would be easy to fix.

"Hmm, that is interesting," she said as she began to look around the room.

She continued, "I think we need to paint this whole wall. And not just this one, but that one, and that one, and that one." She pointed to the kitchen, hallway, and entry way.

And then—no joke—she said, "This would be a great time to refinish all the trim work in the house."

No kidding, she tagged that on. At this point she didn't even remember the thermostat; in fact, I am certain she never even looked at it. All she saw was this incredible opportunity to snooker me into another remodeling project.

While she was saying this, my head was spinning. How could I countermove on this one? Because gentlemen, I am a tired contractor. I understand something she does not: re-staining the trim work in the house is a massive undertaking. We're talking about taking all the trim work off the walls and windows and then bringing the pieces into the garage, sanding them down, staining them, staining them again, putting on a clear coat, and then putting the pieces back up. That's a project that would take a professional about 160 work hours to complete.

And of course, today I am still working through this ridiculous project that has been in progress for about a year. We have half-painted walls, half-stained trim work, but a brand new thermostat. And if you know what that feels like, then you know what it is like to be married to an interior designer and to feel like you have daily bitten off more than you can chew.

I believe that is also what it feels like when we read Jesus' teachings in Luke 14. His words are unbelievably overwhelming. Jesus is giving it to us straight. He's clarifying for us what it actually means to be a follower, a disciple, a man of God. And He doesn't sugarcoat anything.

The Two Requirements

So here are two straight-up, honest, real requirements of what it means to be a disciple of Jesus Christ. And these are not easy to meet.

The first requirement is that we reform our identity around Christ. Please, never forget that. Being a follower of Jesus Christ is all about identity formation. That's all it's about, from beginning to end. Jesus wants us to know this clearly and decisively.

I love the strength of Luke 14:26, which says, "If anyone comes to me and does not hate his own father and mother and wife and children and brothers and sisters, yes, and even his own life, he cannot be my disciple." Do you see how strong Jesus is with his words? That's called exclusivity. "You cannot be my disciple." I think we often miss the punch of what Jesus is saying here—we are so removed from Jesus' time and culture that we really miss what He is saying to these people.

So stay with me for a moment. If we can just travel back in time a couple of thousand years, you would understand that Jesus is cherry-picking from a list, selecting things that were of highest importance to His audience. Remember, these people were a nomadic people, an agricultural people, and very family-centric. Family was everything, all they had. They worshipped as a family, worked as a family, engaged in commerce as a family. Legacy, safety, health care—everything was built into the family unit.

All of their identity came from their family experience. And so Jesus has listed everything that mattered to them, what they identified with most deeply. Jesus understands that the things we value most are the things that are most embedded into our identity. Please catch that.

The things that we value most are the things that are most embedded into our identity. And it is our identity that Jesus is after.

Turn back to the beginning of the Bible to see this principle play out in the life of Abraham. This is perhaps one of the greatest stories ever told. God comes to Abraham and says,

"I will surely bless you, and I will surely multiply your offspring as the stars of heaven and as the sand that is on the seashore. And your offspring shall possess the gate of his enemies, and in your offspring shall all the nations of the earth be blessed, because you have obeyed my voice." (Genesis 22:17–18)

And Abraham waits for a son to be born as the firstfruits of that prophecy—and he keeps on waiting until he is about 100 years of age, which sounds like an exhausting age to have a kid, but finally, Isaac is born. And then when Isaac turns about 20 years of age, God commands Abraham to do the unthinkable. He tells Abraham to take his son up to Mount Moriah and offer Isaac as a sacrifice to Him. And Abraham just gets up and goes.

What is God doing in that moment? I have often asked myself what He was thinking. Well, God was commanding

RESOLUTE

Abraham to do the same thing that Jesus tells us Luke 14. He's cherry-picking the thing that Abraham could potentially value over his relationship with God—his only son, the child of the promise. And we know of course that the story ends beautifully, but it's horrific up until that point. When Abraham raises the knife toward his son, we witness something that is both horrifying and beautiful at the same time. We learn that God examined Abraham's motivation and saw that he valued nothing over God. Not God's promises, not his son, but God Himself.

What God demanded of Abraham—and what Jesus demands of His followers—is called identify formation. And God intends to drop us right into the middle of that painstaking and sacrificial process.

In Luke 14, Jesus is cherry-picking for His audience in items of importance to them, but if Jesus were speaking directly to us today, I assume He would pick a different list. Career, education, 401K, residence, security, personal entertainment—I think He would ask us the same difficult question, "Do you value these things over Me?" And while we might be inclined to quickly answer "No," I think we should stop to evaluate how we actually think and behave. Because over time, these things we value slowly become embedded into our identity, often without us being aware. I believe most of us would have a hard time facing life without a home, a 401k, our various entertainment options, a decent education, and all our toys. And God wants us to submit those things to Him. All these things we need, God wants—and He'll faithfully and painfully chip away at these idols until all that is left is our love for Him, and His for us.

I work with men all the time, and because of that I speak to counselors quite frequently. And I have to tell you, as I talk with counselors about the kind of issues that men generally face, they tell me that one of the major reasons that a man will seek out counseling is because he's lost his job. His life has come completely undone, because the things that he values most are the things that are attached to his career. And when his career is ripped away, he doesn't know where to go, how to live, or who he even is. Even his home life is transformed, as he either fears or senses resentment from his family.

And you know what that is called? That's called identity formation. That's where God starts to take the things from us that we value most, so that we will turn our heart toward Him. And let's be honest, we need God to bring us to this place where all the idols of our life are stripped away and we become completely reliant on God. This is a great spot for us to be; it just doesn't feel all that great sometimes.

And that is what Jesus is talking about in this text. He's talking about the our core identity, and all the big and small idols that come into our life and take over. And gentlemen, Jesus wants all of your heart, which means all idols must be destroyed. It's crystal clear that what Jesus wants from you is anything that's going to get in the way of your relationship with Him.

It's more comfortable to imagine the Christian life as a nice little thermostat upgrade, but God wants the whole house. He wants to redesign everything, transforming you into a true follower of Jesus Christ. Please hear this—your role in this process is to submit yourself daily to identity formation. This is what God wants most: you. Only you. All of you. And the men that experience the most growth are the ones that generously and willingly submit themselves to the identity formation process.

The second requirement of discipleship is self-denial. Now, this is where Jesus' message continues to build. Going back to Luke 9:51, we see that Jesus "sets his face toward

Jerusalem," determined to complete His redemptive mission of death and resurrection.

And from this point in Luke 9, we see a shift where Jesus' message becomes more direct, His tone gets stronger, the commands become harder, and He speaks plainly about HImself instead of being elusive. He even appears to be a bit short-tempered at times. With His identity out in the open, Jesus is going to be crystal clear about being the requirements of being His disciple.

So Jesus says this: "Whoever does not bear his own cross and come after me cannot be my disciple" (Luke 14:27).

To set this in context, remember that Jesus had performed numerous miracles at this point—significantly more than the Gospels could document, according to John. Large crowds of people flocked to Jesus because they were enamored with Him as their potential Messiah and political savior. They thought He was headed to Jerusalem to establish a political kingdom. And Jesus, in the middle of His journey to Jerusalem turns to them and says, "It's not about a crown. It's about a cross."

The crowd must have been completely bewildered. I mean, completely baffled by this whole speech. They didn't understand what He was talking about, as the rest of the story makes clear. Skipping ahead in the narrative, we see that no one's hanging out at the cross with Jesus except for a few select family members and believers. Everyone else is gone. Why? Because they couldn't accept the reality of Jesus' mission. They wanted no part of the cross.

By preaching the true requirements of discipleship, Jesus does something few pastors would dare attempt. Most pastors want to grow the church they lead by attracting crowds and building infrastructure to sustain ongoing attendance. But Jesus wanted disciples, not followers. He was willing to thin the crowds for the sake of clarifying the cost of discipleship. And I'm thankful that he did that here, because now we, too, have a better understanding of what being a disciple really means.

Unfortunately, Jesus' audience in Luke 14 had a crown/cross contradiction going on in their minds. This cross concept completely conflicted with their understanding of a redeeming king. Which leads to the question: If we don't understand Jesus' ultimate call to self-denial, do we really understand what we've gotten ourselves into as a follower of Jesus Christ? Despite Jesus' effort to clarify the matter for us, I think we too often misunderstand the call to self-denial. Similar to the crown/cross contradiction, we suffer from a Savior/Lord contradiction. Let's take a look at what that means.

The Savior-Lord Contradiction

We love the idea of a Savior. We love it. It is the most fantastic idea ever. You are in the pit of your sin, and you want to get out? How about a Savior! He will save you from the condemnation of your own sin. That is good stuff, men. Because our list of sin is really long. I know mine is, and you know the truth about yourself. We love the idea of a Savior who will save us from our circumstances, from the pit of Hell, and from eternal damnation. So we love the idea of a crown. We love it!

We love the idea of mercy and love washing over us. Forgiveness and grace—we love these spiritual blessings. And typically we make a profession of faith because of this. People like me convince you of all the blessings of being a follower of Christ and you buy in.

But for some reason we fail to communicate to you about the other side of a relationship with Christ. Jesus is Lord. As

Lord, He expects your allegiances in a life of complete self-denial. You need to place yourself at the feet of Jesus Christ and allow Him to lead you for the rest of your life. Which means you're going to have to deny self for the rest of your days on earth.

That's a hard message that we don't often hear, but this is exactly what Jesus Christ wants people to learn from this text. To reach the crown, you first have to bear the cross that Jesus calls you to carry. Whatever that burden looks like, whatever that difficulty is, you must be faithful for the rest of your life. Jesus calls us to embrace the cross, to take it willingly in the same way He embraced His. Once we obey, we discover that our suffering, too, is redemptive and purposeful. We find that the cross and the crown are entwined. But this means that quite a bit rides on our obedience: to reject the cross is to forfeit the crown. Will you suffer in this world or the next?

So what does the Christian life mean to you? Is it about a crown alone, or is it also about a cross? In case there is any question in your mind, Jesus clarifies for us exactly what discipleship entails. To be a disciple, you must let God reconstruct your identity based solely on love for Him, while submitting to a life-long process of self-denial. That's it.

Closing and Convincing Arguments

Now, after Jesus shared this message, He put a little exclamation point on it with three anecdotal stories. The first was a story about a builder, the second drew from military warfare, and the third story was about the nature of salt.

First, the story of the builder:

"For which of you, desiring to build a tower, does not first sit down and count the cost, whether he has enough to complete it? Otherwise, when he has laid a foundation and

is not able to finish, all who see it begin to mock him, saying, 'This man began to build and was not able to finish.'"
(Luke 14: 28–30)

If you're in the construction industry, you fully understand what Jesus intended to communicate. If you start a project and you don't finish, what you've built is a monument to your own shame. If you would like to see one, just come over to my house and I'll show you my long-unfinished paint-and-stain project. If you've ever left a project undone, you know how this feels.

But there's a key difference between an abandoned work of construction and a work in progress, even if both look similar on the surface. The sort of work that God wants to do in our hearts takes a long time. A lifetime, in fact. I may look at my half-painted house and feel shame, but my wife hasn't forgotten the vision she had way back when she first saw the new thermostat. She in turn won't let me forget her vision for the house, and won't let me leave the project unfinished. It may take another ten years at this rate—though she's always nudging me to move faster—but we'll get there. And in the same way, God doesn't give up on the vision He has for us. He'll urge us forward when we grow weary from the process, and remind us of the perfection of His designs when all we see are the raw materials. We have everything we need to succeed, but we must be faithful.

Jesus' point is that being a disciple is all about refusing to abandon the work. Consider the Parable of the Soils found in Matthew 7. A man sprinkled seeds on four types of soil; three initially nurtured a seedling, but only one brought it to maturity.

So the raw application is this: don't get into identity formation and self-denial unless you're going to see it through. Jesus could have said it this way: "Follow Me if you're going all the way; otherwise, don't bother."

Next, an illustration from military warfare. This anecdote is a little more cryptic.

"Or what king, going out to encounter another king in war, will not sit down first and deliberate whether he is able with ten thousand to meet him who comes against him with twenty thousand? And if not, while the other is yet a great way off, he sends a delegation and asks for terms of peace."
(Luke 14:31–32)

This one is fascinating and it's taken me years to understand it. So what you've got here is a king, and he goes to war with an opposing king. And as the war begins, he realizes that he doesn't have the military resources to win, so he considers the potential losses and decides to ask for terms of peace. Here's what I think Jesus means: At the end of time, when you come against the King of Judgment, you're going to lose. So it's better to ask for terms of peace now, because you are in a losing battle against this King. Don't wait until Judgment Day to engage with Him. You can surrender now or suffer later. You've got to choose between temporal suffering and eternal suffering, but just a heads up—you will not win against God.

And then finally the nice little bow at the end, and I love this one—it's about salt. Guys, I love salt! My wife hates this about me. My favorite salt comes in those packets from McDonald's. I love those little packets. Ultra-fine, and it sticks nicely to every fry.

"Salt is good, but if salt has lost its taste, how shall its saltiness be restored? It is of no use either for the soil or for the manure pile. It is thrown away. He who has ears to hear, let him hear."
(Luke 14:34–35)

In Jesus' culture, salt was very valuable. It was useful for healing, preserving, and seasoning. In many cases it was even more valuable than gold. But what was especially interesting is that Roman soldiers were paid in salt. It's a word from which we derive the word "salary." Therefore the use of the word "salt" in this text implies value, since salt was an item of intrinsic and extrinsic value. And in these closing words, Jesus is saying, "You can either invest your life in things of intrinsic and extrinsic value, or you can be useless. But remember that while even manure has use and value, an unsalty person has none. Don't throw away your value, because you are of great worth to the kingdom."

So Jesus takes a difficult message and says, "Yes, it's difficult—but why wouldn't you invest yourself into something of this much value?" Why not launch yourself into a life of identity formation and do the hard thing? It's the most valuable choice that you will ever make in life.

Your Challenge

My hope is that this book will encourage you to take a deliberate step toward conviction and see the value in living a life fully devoted to Jesus Christ. That you would take a willing step into conviction as a disciple, and start living out the calling that Jesus Christ gives to each of us as men. Because Jesus Christ didn't just preach conviction—He lived it out. He modeled it for us, for He was "the man" that we all have failed to be.

These teachings should move you from being convicted as a man of God to actually living with conviction as God's man. And I hope you have learned that Jesus' definition for manhood is more about living obediently with conviction than about being ruggedly masculine. Unfortunately, the word man is a very broken word and often devoid of real meaning. I have often wondered if phrases like "man up" or "grow up and be a man" are simply failed attempts to communicate something more about the purpose that we grasp for, but do not fully comprehend. After all, this has been true since the beginning of time. Adam blew his attempt at godly manhood pretty early in the creation story, but then came Jesus, the second Adam, who displayed what it really meant to be "the man" (1 Corinthians 15:45–49).

We have a man problem, not a church problem.

And please keep in mind, we do not have a church problem, we have a man problem! I too often hear men complain about their church, and the problem always seems to lie with politics, pastors, strategies, the building, funding campaigns, and the like. But men, our church issues are not solved with better church strategies, bigger buildings, or more money. Our church issues are tackled one person at a time, one sin at a time, and one conviction at a time, one man at a time. And thus the reason for writing this book.

I hope to draw out other men who will join with me in saying, "Let's live with conviction regardless of the cost for the glory of Christ." These are the men with whom I want to partner and build and serve. Men who are all-in. Men who live guided by biblical codes and convictions. Men who call out in a strong voice with no hesitation to God, "I am Your man, and I will stand in the breach."

Gentlemen, join me in the journey of becoming a man of conviction. I would love to do this with you. Stand with me in the breach.

*Give me one hundred men who fear
nothing but sin and desire nothing but
God, and I care not whether they be
clergyman or laymen, they alone will shake
the gates of Hell and set up the kingdom
of Heaven upon the earth.*

John Wesley

RESOLUTE

The Resolute Organization

Resolute is a Christian men's discipleship and leadership development organization. We provide Cohort experiences for men as a means to develop them into disciples and leaders who live with conviction in their homes, workplaces, and churches. Resolute Cohort participants engage in a twelve-month experience in a cohort (small group) of 12 to 15 members. They are conducted in weekly 90-minute sessions, led by a trained Resolute Facilitator with years of leadership and ministry experience. Cohorts tackle major biblical and leadership topics through inductive study methods and frameworks and live discussion. Payoffs of the Resolute Cohort program are both tangible and intangible. Overall, Resolute participants see great benefits in the following areas:

- Structured, consistent, and supportive community with other Christian men.
- Improved ability to access, understand, and share truth from the Bible.
- Increased spiritual disciplines and awareness.
- Enhanced connections between faith and everyday life.
- Weekly accountability and challenges that incite growth.

You can engage in a Resolute Cohort with an on-site Associate, or you can engage online through Resolute Virtual using video curriculum. Here are links to our program and lesson sequence.

The Resolute Virtual Cohort

HTTPS://BERESOLUTE.ORG/VIRTUAL/

This is a video-based cohort experience led by an on-site volunteer in your church. This uses our complete discipleship and leadership training curriculum, but you provide the host for the group. This experience is instructed by our founder Vince Miller.

The Resolute Cohort

HTTPS://BERESOLUTE.ORG/RESOLUTE-COHORTS/

This is an Associate-led model using our discipleship and leadership training curriculum. This is our premium model and requires an on-site Associate for weekly meetings over a one-year period.

The Resolute Curriculum

HTTPS://BERESOLUTE.ORG/RESOLUTE-CONTENT/

This wire frame represents the 48 lessons we tackle over the course of one year. This is a full, robust curriculum.

The Resolute Podcast App

HTTPS://BERESOLUTE.ORG/

On our home page you will find a link to our App. Here you will find Men's Small Group Material not contained in the training curriculum. This is additional material to supplement any men's group in your church.

Use the Resolute System

HTTPS://BERESOLUTE.ORG/COMMITMENT/

Just like in the last chapter you will find at this web address the following resources:

- A printable Resolute Small Group Guide that supports this chapter.
- Access to an Audio Podcast and Video Curriculum that give you ready-made content for your men's group.

RESOLUTE